Being
Honest
with God
and Others

# AUTHENTICITY

**Interactions Small Group Series**

*Authenticity: Being Honest with God and Others*
*Character: Reclaiming Six Endangered Qualities*
*Commitment: Developing Deeper Devotion to Christ*
*Community: Building Relationships within God's Family*
*Essential Christianity: Practical Steps for Spiritual Growth*
*Fruit of the Spirit: Living the Supernatural Life*
*Getting a Grip: Finding Balance in Your Daily Life*
*Jesus: Seeing Him More Clearly*
*Lessons on Love: Building Deeper Relationships*
*Living in God's Power: Finding God's Strength for Life's Challenges*
*Love in Action: Experiencing the Joy of Serving*
*Marriage: Building Real Intimacy*
*Meeting God: Psalms for the Highs and Lows of Life*
*New Identity: Discovering Who You Are in Christ*
*Parenting: How to Raise Spiritually Healthy Kids*
*Prayer: Opening Your Heart to God*
*Reaching Out: Sharing God's Love Naturally*
*The Real Deal: Discover the Rewards of Authentic Relationships*
*Significance: Understanding God's Purpose for Your Life*
*Transformation: Letting God Change You from the Inside Out*

InterActions
small group series

Being
Honest
with God
and Others

# AUTHENTICITY

## BILL HYBELS

WITH KEVIN AND SHERRY HARNEY

ZONDERVAN™

GRAND RAPIDS, MICHIGAN 49530 USA

WILLOW
Willow Creek Resources

We want to hear from you. Please send your comments about this book to us in care of zreview@zondervan.com. Thank you.

*Authenticity*
Copyright © 1996 by Willow Creek Association

Requests for information should be addressed to:

Zondervan, *Grand Rapids, Michigan 49530*

ISBN-10: 0-310-26588-6
ISBN-13: 978-0-310-26588-7

*Interior Design by Rick Devon and Michelle Espinoza*

*Printed in the United States of America*

05 06 07 08 09 10 11 12 /❖ DCI/ 10 9 8 7 6 5 4 3 2 1

# Contents

# INTERACTIONS

In 1992, Willow Creek Community Church, in partnership with Zondervan and the Willow Creek Association, released a curriculum for small groups entitled the Walking with God series. In just three years, almost a half million copies of these small group study guides were being used in churches around the world. The phenomenal response to this curriculum affirmed the need for relevant and biblical small group materials.

At the writing of this curriculum, there are nearly 3,000 small groups meeting regularly within the structure of Willow Creek Community Church. We believe this number will increase as we continue to place a central value on small groups. Many other churches throughout the world are growing in their commitment to small group ministries as well, so the need for resources is increasing.

In response to this great need, the Interactions small group series has been developed. Willow Creek Association and Zondervan have joined together to create a whole new approach to small group materials. These discussion guides are meant to challenge group members to a deeper level of sharing, create lines of accountability, move followers of Christ into action, and help group members become fully devoted followers of Christ.

## SUGGESTIONS FOR INDIVIDUAL STUDY

1. Begin each session with prayer. Ask God to help you understand the passage and to apply it to your life.
2. A good modern translation, such as the New International Version, the New American Standard Bible, or the New Revised Standard Version will give you the most help. Questions in this guide are based on the New International Version.
3. Read and reread the passage(s). You must know what the passage says before you can understand what it means and how it applies to you.
4. Write your answers in the spaces provided in the study guide. This will help you to express clearly your understanding of the passage.
5. Keep a Bible dictionary handy. Use it to look up unfamiliar words, names, or places.

## Suggestions for Group Study

1. Come to the session prepared. Careful preparation will greatly enrich your time in group discussion.
2. Be willing to join in the discussion. The leader of the group will not be lecturing, but will encourage people to discuss what they have learned in the passage. Plan to share what God has taught you in your individual study.
3. Stick to the passage being studied. Base your answers on the verses being discussed rather than on outside authorities such as commentaries or your favorite author or speaker.
4. Try to be sensitive to the other members of the group. Listen attentively when they speak, and be affirming whenever you can. This will encourage more hesitant members of the group to participate.
5. Be careful not to dominate the discussion. By all means participate! But allow others to have equal time.
6. If you are the discussion leader, you will find additional suggestions and helpful ideas in the leader's notes.

## Additional Resources and Teaching Materials

At the end of this study guide you will find a collection of resources and teaching materials to help you in your growth as a follower of Christ. You will also find resources that will help your church develop and build fully devoted followers of Christ.

# Introduction:
# Being Honest with
# God and Others

A personal growth conference for Christians isn't the place where you would expect to see a fight. Especially a fight between leaders. But at just such a conference I faced the unexpected. As a young Christian, I was just beginning to learn about leadership. Getting a chance to observe how mature Christians behaved was just what I needed. Or so I thought.

Midway through the meeting, a question over a delicate decision led to a debate. Debating descended to arguing and finally to ugly division. It took only forty-five minutes for these "mature" Christians to nearly come to blows.

Before those gathered could resolve the issue, however, the signal came for the next part of the conference schedule—a worship service. Everyone shuffled to an adjoining room, where the committee chairman, who had been as argumentative as anyone else in the previous meeting, grabbed the microphone. Smiling from ear to ear, he said, "Scripture tells us that the mark of a true Christian is love, so let's all join hands and sing, 'They Will Know We Are Christians by Our Love.'"

That was my initiation into the world of inauthentic Christianity. I've learned that such inconsistency is not uncommon. People too often live one way when the spotlights are on and another way behind closed doors.

The dictionary defines *authentic* as "something that conforms to what it is represented or claimed to be." Authenticity means consistency—between words and actions, and between claimed values and actual priorities. Inauthenticity occurs when we claim to be one thing, then prove to be something else.

Years ago I read a story about a small community that had a gigantic oak tree in the middle of its town square. The tree was the pride of the townspeople. It had been there long before most of them were born and would undoubtedly outlive them. Then one day storm winds cracked the tree in half, revealing a trunk filled with disease. A symbol of strength on the outside, the oak had been weak and vulnerable on the inside. For years it had fooled its unknowing admirers.

That story still haunts me.

I believe the greatest challenge facing the church is the disease eating away at its power and integrity—inauthentic Christianity. In the pulpits and in the pews, there are too many inconsistent Christians.

Inauthentic Christianity manifests itself in many ways. In this series we will examine six of those manifestations. We will study inconsistent Christian living in

1. a style of Christianity based more on external methods than on internal change, an attempt at godliness that lacks the power;
2. relationships marked more by deception than honest dialogue;
3. misguided Christians who hide heartache and grief behind smiling masks;
4. Christians who evangelize out of guilt;
5. workers whose jobs are drudgery rather than meaningful labor, or obsessions rather than professions;
6. budgets that are out of control because Christians don't take stewardship seriously.

Christianity is meant to be a supernatural walk with a living, dynamic, speaking, personal God. Why then do so many Christians live inconsistent, powerless lives?

Authentic Christianity begins with spiritual authenticity—a vital, daily relationship with Jesus Christ. But a vital relationship with Jesus takes time—not leftover, throwaway time, but quality time for solitude, contemplation, and reflection. In this series of interactions we will discover what it means to live authentic lives as fully devoted followers of Christ.

*Bill Hybels*

# A New Dimension in Spirituality

## THE BIG PICTURE

I backed the car out of the driveway as I do every morning at 5:45. I switched the radio from a program on ethics to the Tokyo stock closing, and drove through the neighboring sub-division, mentally critiquing architectural designs. I bought coffee at the twenty-four-hour coffee shop and successfully avoided the talkative cashier. As I turned onto the church campus, I formulated a convincing defense for a ministry plan that I hoped the staff would adopt. I climbed to my third-floor office, wondering about the productivity of the nighttime maintenance crew. I shuffled through the mountain of mail on my desk and wished someone else could answer it.

I spun my chair around and looked out the window at the church lake steaming in the crispness of the morning. In that quiet moment I saw the previous quarter hour for what it had been—time tainted by purely human perspective. Not once during that time had I seen the world through godly eyes. I had been more interested in international finances than in the moral demise of our nation. I had thought more about houses than the people inside them. I had considered the tasks awaiting me more important than the woman who served my coffee. I had been more intent on logically supporting my plans than sincerely seeking God's. I'd thought more about staff members' productivity than their walk with the Lord or their family life.

I'd viewed correspondence as drudgery rather than a way to offer encouragement, counsel, or help.

It was 6:00 A.M., and I needed a renewed heart and mind. Like a compass out of adjustment, my thoughts and feelings were pointing in the wrong direction. They needed to be recalibrated—to be realigned with God's accurate, perfect perspective.

You see, in the space of a day, your relationship with Jesus Christ can fall from the heights to the depths, from vitality to superficiality, from life-changing interaction to meaningless ritual. That's a humbling admission, but it's true. In a mere twenty-four hours, you can slide from spiritual authenticity into spiritual inauthenticity.

## A WIDE ANGLE VIEW

**1** How have you seen yourself slide into patterns of inauthenticity?

*What factors contribute to this slide?*

## A BIBLICAL PORTRAIT

Read Psalm 46

**2** This psalm clearly addresses the stress and strain of living in this world. In eleven short verses we read about troubles, cosmic chaos, earthquakes, conflict among the nations, kingdoms falling, and the reality of war. After this list of life's turmoil, the psalmist writes: "Be still, and know that I am God; I will be exalted among the nations, I will be exalted in the earth" (v. 10). How is it possible to "be still" in the middle of a life filled with busyness and stress?

*Tell about a time you found a quiet place in God even when the world around you was like a raging storm.*

## SHARPENING THE FOCUS

Read Snapshot "Put It in Writing"

### PUT IT IN WRITING

Over the years, as I've traveled and spoken at churches and conferences, I've occasionally met leaders who somehow seemed to avoid the daily slide into artificial Christianity. Whenever I could, I asked what their secret was. In almost every case they said "journaling"—the daily process of examining and evaluating their lives in written form.

Now, if you think I heard that and ran right out to buy a journal, you're dead wrong; I thought the idea was ridiculous. People who had time for journaling were not like me. They didn't have my schedule or live with my kind of pressure. Still, I had to admit that too often I repeated the same mistakes again and again. Too often I went to bed with regrets about my actions. Too often I made decisions inconsistent with my professed values. In a rare moment of honesty, I faced the fact that I was living under the tyranny of an unexamined life.

At that time I was chaplain for the Chicago Bears. Occasionally before the Monday morning Bible study, I'd join them while they watched films and did postgame analysis. They would go over every play of the previous day's game so they could learn from their mistakes and not repeat them in the next game.

Finally, I understood. The journalers were simply telling me to *do a postgame analysis!* How could I expect to be conformed to the image of Christ without evaluating my mistakes and progress? How could I grow without examining my character, decision-making, ministry, marriage, and child-rearing? Maybe journaling *was* for me.

3 What is your first response to my suggestion to journal as a means of examining and evaluating your life?

Read Snapshot "Yesterday"

## YESTERDAY

After I was convinced of the value of journaling, I was still worried about facing a blank sheet of paper, until a well-known author offered a simple suggestion: Buy a spiral notebook and restrict yourself to *one page a day.* Every day, start with the word "Yesterday." Write a brief description of people you met with, decisions you made, thoughts or feelings you had, high points, low points, frustrations, Bible-reading—anything about the previous day. Then *analyze it.* Did you make good decisions or bad ones? Did you use your time wisely or waste it? Should you have done anything differently? Were you authentic in how you lived your life or inauthentic? Journaling can become a chance for daily honesty and learning.

4 Using the space provided, take no more than five minutes to try journaling. Use the guidelines given in the above Snapshot "Yesterday." Don't try to be overly deep or profound; simply write about what you did yesterday and allow yourself to examine your day.

*What did you learn about yourself through this brief experience of journaling?*

Read Snapshot "Now What?"

### NOW WHAT?

The only problem with slowing down and meeting with God was that I realized I didn't have much to say. The second part of my path to spiritual authenticity—my prayer life—was amazingly weak, and had been for years. Then a friend suggested I begin writing out my prayers using a simple outline that would help me stay focused. I try to use this simple outline, called A.C.T.S., each day in my personal prayers.

*Adoration*—Each morning, after filling your "Yesterday" page, write a big "A" on the next page. Then spend a few minutes writing a paragraph of praise to the Lord. Paraphrase a psalm or attempt to write a poem. Or focus on the attributes of God, sometimes listing many, sometimes meditating on just one.

*Confession*—One way to make confession genuine and effective is to write out specific sins. Do you know what it's like to see your sins in print? Try writing something like this: "Last night I told Todd I would play ball with him, but I didn't keep my word. I lied to my son." It's so easy to justify our behavior by saying, "I intended to play ball. It just didn't work out." Instead, we need to see our sins for what they are.

*Thanksgiving*—In this section of your journal, thank God for answered prayers and for specific spiritual, relational, and material blessings. Almost everything in life fits under one of those categories. By the time you finish your list, you'll be ready to go back to adoration.

*Supplication*—Break your requests into four categories: ministry, people, family, and personal. Or make up your own categories of prayer. Keep a list of what you've prayed about. After a few weeks, look back over it. You'll be amazed at what God has done.

# 5

Use the space provided below to write out your prayer using the A.C.T.S. outline explained above.

*Adoration:*

*Confession:*

*Thanksgiving:*

*Supplication:*

*What is one characteristic of God you wrote down in the adoration section of your prayer, and why did you choose this quality?*

*How does it make you feel to see your sins in writing?*

*What are you thanking God for today?*

*What have you listed under the supplication section that you would like your small group members to be aware of and pray for you?*

Read Snapshot "Listening"

---

## LISTENING

Journaling and writing out my prayers slow me down enough to hear God's still, small voice. The third step in my daily discipline is to listen and ask God to speak to me.

Scripture says, "Be still, and know that I am God" (Ps. 46:10). It's these quiet moments after prayer that really matter. They nourish authentic Christianity. Power flows out of stillness, strength out of solitude. Decisions that change the course of lives come out of these quiet times.

Begin with these words: "Lord, You talked to Your children all through history, and You said You're an unchangeable God. Talk to me now. I'm listening. I'm open."

Then I ask four questions. I never hear an audible voice, but I often get impressions that are so strong and real I write them down. In these quiet moments I ask:

- What is my next step in my relationship with you?
- What's the next step in the development of my character?
- What's the next step in my family life?
- What's the next step in my ministry?

You might ask other questions: What's the next step in my vocation? In my dating relationship? In my education?

Over time, you'll become more adept at sensing God's answers to these questions. You'll receive Scripture verses, ideas, or insights that are just what you need. Those moments of inspiration will become precious memories you carry with you all day.

---

6 As you take time for silence and listening, use the space below to write any impressions or direction you feel God is giving you.

*What was your experience during this time of listening?*

7 We have experimented with journaling, focused prayer (A.C.T.S.), and listening. What kind of commitment do you want to make to develop one, two, or all of these prayer disciplines in your life in the coming month?

*What can your small group members do to encourage you and keep you accountable?*

## PUTTING YOURSELF IN THE PICTURE

### BUYING A JOURNAL AND USING IT

Take time in the next day or two to buy a journal. A simple spiral or three-ring binder will do. On the first page, write down your commitment to how often you will be making time to be with God. Will you be journaling, using the A.C.T.S. prayer, listening and writing down God's answers, keeping notes on your personal Bible study? Be specific with your goals. Now, start doing it! Look back once a week to evaluate what you have been learning and how God has been shaping you into an authentic follower of Jesus.

### TEACHING WHAT YOU HAVE LEARNED

Through this session, you have learned three different ways to grow in your faith and become a more fully devoted follower of Christ. Take time in the coming week to sit down with another Christian and tell them what you have learned so they can also grow in spiritual authenticity. Once you have communicated what you have learned, ask them to help keep you accountable and let them know if they want to make a similar commitment, you will pray for them and help keep them accountable also.

# TRUTH-TELLING: THE PATHWAY TO AUTHENTIC RELATIONSHIPS

## REFLECTIONS FROM SESSION 1

1. If you have been journaling over the past week or two, how has this experience made your prayer life more authentic?
2. What would you say to encourage other people to develop the discipline of journaling and writing out their prayers?
3. If you took time to tell someone else about journaling, the A.C.T.S. prayer, or listening, how did they respond? If you have developed an accountability partner outside your small group, tell your group members how this support network is helping you grow in an authentic prayer life.

## THE BIG PICTURE

We all yearn for relationships where we can be completely honest, open, and vulnerable. Where we can share failures as well as successes, shortcomings as well as strengths. Where we can reveal doubts and fears. Where we can find empathy and confidentiality.

These intimate, authentic relationships are exactly what God has in mind for us. He created us for relationships and wants us to experience them at their best.

Over the years, I have had people inform me they don't need such relationships. But they've been unconvincing. Their overdone bravado has always struck me as a poor cover-up for their disappointments in building good relationships.

All of us long for deep, authentic relationships marked by integrity and open communication, but how often do we experience them? Occasionally? Once in a lifetime? Never?

During the last decade and a half, I've heard many tales of relationships marred by hidden hostilities and unspoken hurts. While a number of factors contribute to this, I believe the biggest problem is that too often we violate the basic requirement of authentic relationships: honesty. Learning how to tell others the truth is the basis of genuine relationships and the goal of this session.

## A WIDE ANGLE VIEW

1  What are some characteristics of an authentic relationship?

*Why do you see these characteristics as valuable?*

A U T H E N T I C I T Y

## A BIBLICAL PORTRAIT

Read Ephesians 4:14–16, 25

**2** The apostle Paul calls us to be "speaking the truth in love" and to "put off falsehood and speak truthfully." How is truth-telling a sign of maturity in a relationship?

## SHARPENING THE FOCUS

Read Snapshot "A Great Theory, but . . ."

---

### A GREAT THEORY, BUT . . .

"...if I told my boss the truth, he would blow his stack."

"...if I told my husband how I feel about his constant traveling, he would get defensive and withdraw even more."

"...if I told my parents how frustrated I am in school, they would be too disappointed to understand."

"...if I told my wife how sexually frustrated I am in our marriage, she would accuse me of having a one-track mind."

"...if I told my professor the real reason I didn't finish my paper on time, she would dock my grade."

On and on we go, explaining why we can't afford to tell the truth.

Few of us debate the biblical position on truth-telling. Speak the truth in love. Don't bear false witness. Lay aside falsehood and speak truth to one another. (See Eph. 4:15; Ex. 20:16; Eph. 4:25.) We agree in theory that honesty is the best policy. It's the key to authentic relationships.

But in those awkward moments when we stand face-to-face with someone, knowing they may not readily receive the truth, truth-telling doesn't sound like such a great idea. It might be okay for someone else, but not for us.

---

**3** Using an incident in your own life, describe what happened when you decided to:

- "keep the peace" instead of telling the truth

- tell the truth, and it resulted in damage to the relationship

- tell the truth, and it resulted in healing and a more authentic relationship

Read Snapshot "Enter the Tunnel"

---

### ENTER THE TUNNEL

In his book *The Different Drum*, Scott Peck presents an interesting theory about relationships. He says God designed us to yearn for open, honest, authentic relationships—"communal" relationships. But because we choose peacekeeping over truth-telling, we end up in "pseudocommunal" relationships instead.

Pseudocommunal relationship are marriages, family relationships, or friendships that are strictly at a surface level. No one says anything "unsafe." People in these relationships never discuss misunderstandings, reveal hurt feelings, air frustrations, or ask difficult questions. The underlying rule in pseudocommunity is "Don't rock the boat. Don't disturb the peace."

But it's a counterfeit peace. Misunderstandings arise, but are never resolved. Feelings beg to be shared, but are kept hidden. Offenses occur, but nobody talks about them. Doubts about integrity creep in, but are never dealt with.

In time, such relationships deteriorate. The secret agendas of hurt and misunderstanding lead to detachment, distrust, and bitterness. Feelings of love begin to die. It's the story of too many marriages, family relationships, and friendships.

Peck says the only antidote to pseudocommunity is chaos—I call it "the tunnel of chaos"—where hurts are unburied, hostilities revealed, and tough questions asked. Skiers know that if they want to drive from Denver to Vail, Colorado, they have to go through the Eisenhower Tunnel. It doesn't matter how much they dislike tunnels; if they want to make it to Vail, they have to go through that tunnel. Likewise, no matter how unpleasant the tunnel of chaos is, there's no other route to authentic relationships.

---

**4** Picture one current relationship where you need to enter the "tunnel of chaos" if you are going to move toward authenticity. What is keeping you from entering the tunnel?

**5** What are some of the risks you must take when you enter the tunnel and move toward honest communication?

*What are some of the consequences of refusing to enter the tunnel and choosing to live in pseudocommunity?*

Read Snapshot "Have You Seen This Person?"

## HAVE YOU SEEN THIS PERSON?

In our effort to build authentic relationships, sometimes we try to take shortcuts. Rather than go through the tunnel of chaos, we try other methods of communication. Ask yourself if you recognize any of these characters:

*Henry the Hint-dropper*—He wants community but tries to build it with carefully placed hints and statements that make his point without ever really saying what is on his mind.

*Mary the Manipulator*—She knows what she wants in her relationships but can't seem to look people in the eye and state what is on her mind. Instead, she nags and pressures others in an effort to get them to conform to what she feels they should be doing.

*Gary the Guilt-tripper*—He likes to use phrases like, "After all I have done for you" and "If you really cared about me, you would . . ." Rather than seek real community, he settles for getting his way through coercion.

*Ivan the Intimidator*—He also wants community, but in his frustration and impatience resorts to pressure tactics, temper tantrums, and even occasional threats. He may get his way, but there is no real authenticity in this kind of relationship.

**6** How have you experienced the use of these (and similar) approaches to avoid truth-telling?

Read Snapshot "Guidelines for Truth-telling"

## GUIDELINES FOR TRUTH-TELLING

Authentic relationships provide some of the greatest joys of life, but we'll never experience them if we play the games just discussed. We need to deal openly with the wedges that occasionally get stuck in even the best relationships.

Here are some practical suggestions for negotiating the tunnel so we can move into true community:

First, *identify the real obstacle*. Before you blurt out an unedited, "Hey, Buddy, I've got a problem with you," take time to determine the real issue. Is it hurt feelings? Is it a history of dishonesty? Do you feel neglected? Misunderstood? Identify the issue, then talk to the Lord about it. Sort it out. Some people find it helpful to organize their thoughts on paper.

Second, *arrange to meet the person face-to-face as soon as possible*. Jesus tells us that if we have a problem in a relationship we should meet with that person in private (Matt. 18:15). Paul says we should do it as soon as possible. "Do not let the sun go down while you are still angry" (Eph. 4:26). The longer we stay in pseudocommunity, the more the relationship deteriorates.

Third, when you meet, *affirm the relationship before you open up the agenda*. If you're meeting with your spouse, say, "Look, honey, I love you and I value our relationship. I want our marriage to be all it can be, and I believe it has the potential to be mutually satisfying in every way. But I need to talk to you about a few things that are standing in the way."

Fourth, *make observations rather than accusations*. Human beings tend to do what animals do when they're attacked: they strike back. Don't put up your dukes and start throwing punches. Say, "Look, I'm feeling hurt by some things you did. You probably didn't intend to hurt me, but that's what I feel. Can we talk about it?" Or "I'm sensing a change in our relationship. I don't feel as comfortable with you anymore. I'd like your input." That opens the way for dialogue that can lead to true community.

7 Why is each step in this process important for safely navigating through the communicational tunnel of chaos?

8 Who is one person you need to begin this process with in the coming days?

*How can you support one another as you each seek authentic communication in your relationship?*

## PUTTING YOURSELF IN THE PICTURE

### IDENTIFYING PSEUDOCOMMUNITY

In this session you discussed some of the patterns of communication that lead to a false sense of community. Take time in the coming week to honestly evaluate your communication and relational skills. Where do you see the unhealthy patterns in your life that are similar to:

- Henry the Hint-dropper
- Mary the Manipulator
- Gary the Guilt-tripper
- Ivan the Intimidator

*What can you do to change your communication patterns and avoid unhealthy trends in your relationships?*

# HONEST EMOTIONS

## REFLECTIONS FROM SESSION 2

1. At the end of the first session in this series of interactions, you were encouraged to honestly evaluate your communication skills and identify any unhealthy patterns. What is one unhealthy pattern you see in your communication and what are you doing to become a truth-teller?

2. What is one relationship that you see growing deeper and more authentic because you are seeking to be a truth-teller?

## THE BIG PICTURE

She was young, attractive, gifted—a devoted wife and mother and a faithful leader in the church. Then her world fell apart. A sudden, inexplicable anxiety became debilitating, and she ended up in the psychiatric ward of a local hospital. Months of intense therapy uncovered the horror of childhood sexual abuse. In a complex and desperate attempt to protect her from the pain of reality, her mind had covered up the truth for years. But now the cover-up was cracking, the truth was oozing out, and the pain was too great to bear.

He was a successful businessman, a beloved father and grandfather, a warm friend, a devout Christian. His only problem was his uncontrolled eating. Diets and exercise programs helped for a while, but always ended in defeat. His excess weight led to discouragement and heart trouble. Finally, a counselor showed him the connection between his compulsive eating habits and the emotional abuse he had experienced in the home of a harsh and insensitive father.

She was the tough, aggressive type—unemotional and independent, confident and self-assured, competent in business and relationships. Sure, there had been disappointments, but they hadn't gotten her down. She suffered none of the usual effects of growing up in a broken home. She had faced job loss, miscarriage, and relational disappointments with calm resignation. She was on top of things—until the tears hit. With no warning, the dam broke. Years of unacknowledged grief consolidated into an overwhelming flood of tears. She thought she had successfully avoided the pain, but in the end the pain won.

Psychologists would tell us that these people are dealing with "unfinished business"—issues from the past that negatively affect their present behavior because they never properly dealt with the problems. Submerged pain. Denied fear. Ignored grief. Experts tell us unfinished business is the source of many of the emotional and relational difficulties we face.

For years, the Christian community has been in debate. The church has been unwilling to believe that concepts like unfinished business have any legitimate relationship to the difficulties Christians face. Many Christian teachers would lead you to believe that the key to success, happiness, and overcoming pain is to get your mind off yourself and on to the Lord. But is this really the road to an authentic emotional life for a Christian?

## A WIDE ANGLE VIEW

1 Tell about a situation in your life in which you are still dealing with unfinished business. When you face emotionally difficult experiences, how do you tend to deal with your pain?

## A BIBLICAL PORTRAIT

Read 2 Corinthians 4:7–12

2 As you read the apostle Paul's words, how would you describe his emotional state and feelings at this time in his life?

*Paul seems to be expressing both honest pain and genuine strength at the same time. How can these two things exist in a person simultaneously?*

## SHARPENING THE FOCUS

Read Snapshot "Rejoice! Rejoice! Rejoice!"

### REJOICE! REJOICE! REJOICE!

Philippians 4:4 says, "Rejoice in the Lord always. I will say it again: Rejoice!" This passage and others like it have caused tremendous confusion in the body of Christ. More than once, I've stood by the side of a believer who's mourning the loss of a loved one and overheard something like this: "Well, Mary, we're praising the Lord with you today. Harold is home with his heavenly Father. He's rejoicing right now with us. Isn't it wonderful to be able to praise God even in this? You are praising God, aren't you, Mary? You're not losing the victory, are you?" Mary mumbles her thanks, then inwardly chastises herself for not being a stronger Christian. Why can't she sing the "Hallelujah Chorus" at her husband's funeral like she's supposed to?

I mean, isn't that what Philippians 4:4 tells her to do? Doesn't it tell her—and us—to rejoice over death, loss, injury, trial, failure, and defeat? Doesn't it tell the elders of our church, who regularly pray with seriously afflicted people, to rejoice over eyes that don't see, limbs that don't function, wombs that are barren, or hearts that are broken? Doesn't it tell them to meet with the grieving and trembling, the broken and beaten down, and chastise them for not "rejoicing always"?

## 3

What is your gut reaction to the statements in the Snapshot you just read?

*What does it mean to rejoice in the Lord always?*

Read Snapshot "Suffer, Suffer, Suffer!"

## SUFFER, SUFFER, SUFFER!

Some people face their pain with a plastic grin, inauthentic emotions, and a booming "Praise the Lord!" no matter what they encounter. This extreme is unhealthy. However, we also need to be aware of the opposite extreme. Some people don't believe at all in this opium called rejoicing. They can't find *anything* praiseworthy in pain. In fact, they leave God out of the picture entirely. Their counsel is to just feel the full force of whatever pain comes their way. "Own your anger," they say. "Explore your violated emotions. Plumb the depths of your heartbreak. Come to grips with how unfair life is and how cruelly you've been treated. And whatever you do, don't mix God-talk into your pain. That only leads to deception."

4 What dangers do we face when we try to leave out the process of dealing with "unfinished business" and personal pain?

*How have you experienced the love of God and the presence of the Holy Spirit as essential to the healing process in your life?*

5 Paul teaches us that we can "rejoice in the Lord always," but we don't have to rejoice in everything that happens to us. In the beginning of your small group, some of your small group members spoke about an area in their lives where they are dealing with unfinished business. What are some areas of that "unfinished business" that still bring pain to your life?

*Is there anything in that experience or anything that has come from that experience that has caused you to rejoice in the Lord? If so, what?*

Read Snapshot "So What Do We Do Now?"

---

## SO WHAT DO WE DO NOW?

 What do we do if we're neck-deep in marital troubles, or child-rearing frustrations, or financial, physical, or vocational difficulties? What do we do if we're carrying around unfinished business that bogs us down in an emotional quagmire? How do we get from that place to authentic rejoicing?

First, *refuse to deny the pain, frustration, or heartache*. Denying our difficulties or pretending they don't debilitate us in various ways is deceitful. Thoughtlessly chanting "Praise the Lord anyway" is not being real. So go beyond that. Drop the hypocrisy and be honest with yourself.

Second, *honestly tell God how you feel*. He can handle your authentic cries of pain and disappointment. He can even help you work through them.

Third, *discuss your pain, disappointment, or heartache with someone else*. I can't tell you how many times people have approached me at church with tears in their eyes to tell me something they've "never told anyone before." Haltingly, they report a childhood incident that still haunts them and makes them feel fearful and insecure. Or they tell how disappointed they are with their marriage and how they've been trying to deny the disappointment and pretend everything is okay. They finish their story and say, "I don't know why, but I feel better now. Maybe now I can talk to my husband (or my wife, or my friend, or my small-group leader) about this."

Fourth, *at times, friends can't help enough*. Sometimes your unfinished business may be so weighty and emotionally debilitating that you need to seek help from a Christian counselor.

---

6 Take some time for quiet and honest reflection. Write down the things that are bringing you stress, pain, and anxiety in your life right now. These may be very current issues or things you have dealt with for many years.

7 Take time to silently talk to God about the areas of pain you wrote down from the question above. Be honest with God. Express any pain, frustration, and even anger you might carry in your heart.

8 As a group, discuss the areas of pain and hurt you feel free to talk about.

*What is one area of pain or anxiety in your life right now?*

*What can you do to seek the healing needed to overcome this pain?*

*What can your group members do to support and help you through this time of healing?*

## PUTTING YOURSELF IN THE PICTURE

### LEARNING FROM THE PSALMS

Take time in the coming weeks to meditate on Psalms 22, 28, 30, and 73. Reflect on the following questions:

- How does each psalm contain an honest and heartfelt expression of pain and struggle?

- How does each psalm express genuine trust in God in the midst of the pain?

- What can you learn about your own honest expression of emotion from each psalm?

# UNSTEREOTYPING EVANGELISM

## REFLECTIONS FROM SESSION 3

1. If you took time to study the psalms suggested in the last session, what did you discover about the freedom we have to express our feelings honestly to God?
2. How has growing in honest prayer impacted your life?

## THE BIG PICTURE

Some people believe making evangelism authentic is about as easy as making a hospital stay fun. Just the thought of evangelism strikes terror in them, awakening unwanted feelings of fear, pressure, and guilt. Most of these people grew up under teachers who overemphasized personal evangelism and established unrealistic expectations.

Years ago I attended a conference where the speaker informed us that if we really loved Jesus Christ, we'd share Christ with three people before we went to bed that night. Nearly everyone in the auditorium signaled their acceptance of his challenge by jumping to their feet. I noted it was nearly 10:00 P.M. and refused to respond to his ridiculous, manipulative appeal. I stayed in my seat—and felt humiliated and guilty.

Other people are introverts who have been repeatedly intimidated by extroverted teachers who can't understand why witnessing to strangers on street corners is such a "stretch" for them. "Don't you *care* about people?" they ask.

Well, I have no intention of loading another burden on your back. Authentic evangelism can actually begin to fill you with anticipation and confidence, not terror. It is not motivated by guilt, but is part of a whole new mind-set built around the belief that every individual has a unique, God-ordained evangelistic style. Each of us can enjoy fruitfulness and freedom in witnessing when using our own particular style.

## A WIDE ANGLE VIEW

**1** Tell the group about a successful experience you have had with evangelism or a disastrous one. What were some of the factors that produced the positive or negative results?

## A BIBLICAL PORTRAIT

Read Luke 15:3–7

**2** What strikes you about Jesus' attitude toward lost people?

*How does the attitude of Jesus compare with your own?*

## SHARPENING THE FOCUS

Read Snapshot "What Motivates You?"

### WHAT MOTIVATES YOU?

Many things motivate us to reach out to seekers with the message of God's love. One of them is what I like to call the "stockpile factor"—the sheer scope of God's blessings in our lives. When mature believers have a proper understanding of their spiritual inheritance, they cannot keep their joy over this fact from spilling into other people's lives. One of the most effective ways to be an evangelist is to manage your life in such a way as to stay mindful of your inheritance in Christ. Stay ever aware of the character of God. Never forget the magnitude of the transformation that has taken strangers and converted them into sons and daughters of God. Live with a profound awareness of the size of your spiritual stockpile. When this happens, it will take very little effort or motivation to reach out to lost people and say, "You need to come and see how wonderful God is."

**3** What are some of the blessings God has given you in your spiritual stockpile and how does the reality of this stockpile act as a motivation for you to tell seekers about Jesus?

**4** What are some of the other motivations for followers of Christ to reach out to seekers?

Read Snapshot "Major in the People Business"

## MAJOR IN THE PEOPLE BUSINESS

"Come, follow me," Jesus said, "and I will make you fishers of men" (Matt. 4:19). With these words, Jesus challenged Peter and Andrew to consider a total world- and life-view transformation, a total change in mind-set.

It's as if Jesus said, "Peter, Andrew, for years your whole life has revolved around fishing: how to find fish, how to catch fish, how to market fish. Every day you discussed ways to become more effective fishermen. You devoted all your gifts, talents, and abilities to the pursuit of more fish. And that was fine—really it was—until now. But hear Me well, fellows, there's something far more important for you to do now. I want you to find new life in Me; I want you to discover what God is up to in this world. I want to train you to become fishers of men."

Jesus wasn't saying there was anything wrong with the fishing business—or the construction business, the food business, the travel business, the insurance business, or the real estate business. We all need to make a living and take our professions seriously for the glory of God. But He wanted to make the point that there's something far more important than catching fish and bringing them to market: capturing the attention of sinful men and women and bringing them to the cross of Christ. When the two concerns go head-to-head, as they inevitably will, Jesus tells us to *major in the people business and minor in the fish business.*

**5** What characterizes the life of a person who majors in the fishing business, and what characterizes the life of a person who majors in the business of reaching people for Christ?

Marks of a person who majors on fishing:

- _____
- _____
- _____

Marks of a person who majors on reaching people for Christ:

- _____
- _____
- _____

*How does your mind-set and lifestyle need to change so you can major more on the pursuit of reaching men, women, and children for Christ?*

**6** How did Jesus model the priority of placing the people business above everything else?

*In what ways does His example impact how you live your life?*

Read Snapshot "What's Your Style?"

---

**WHAT'S YOUR STYLE?**

Vast numbers of sincere Christians dismiss the subject of evangelism because they can't handle the thought of street corner preaching, door knocking, and Bible thumping. They fear that if they ever get serious about spreading the message of Christ, they'll have to become obnoxious or behave in ways that are foreign to them. So they commit themselves to church attendance, Bible reading, prayer, fellowship, giving, and serving, but say a polite "No thanks" to evangelism. What a tragedy for the church—and for lost men and women. I believe such thinking is prompted by a satanic strategy to halt the expansion of the kingdom of God—a strategy that has been extremely effective.

How can we counter it? By understanding that there are many styles of effective evangelism. The truth is, there are people you know who need an evangelist of your exact age, career, and level of spiritual understanding. Your particular personality, background, and interests are just what some seekers need to help them understand who Jesus is.

You don't have to become someone you're not in order to be an effective evangelist. You need to be humble, to be submitted to the Holy Spirit, to be prayerful. Then you simply need to be yourself and respond naturally to the opportunities God sends your way.

---

**7** As you read the following brief definitions of different styles of evangelism, discuss the following questions:

*How do you see this style fitting who you are and how God has wired you?*

*What kind of person could be reached with this style of evangelism?*

*How might a Christ follower develop and use this style to reach seekers?*

*Confrontational Style*—The apostle Peter had a confrontational style of evangelism. In Acts 2:14 he took a stand, saying, "Listen carefully to what I say." Then, in verse 36 he told them they had crucified the wrong man; they had crucified the Son of God. He then exhorted them to repent, pleading, "Save yourselves from this corrupt generation" (v. 40).

This confrontational style was a frontal assault. It required confidence and courage. And it was effective! Over three thousand people trusted Christ after Peter shared the Gospel. Some people will be reached only when they are confronted courageously and straightforwardly with the message of Christ. Thankfully, some people are uniquely gifted by God to be able to use a confrontational style of evangelism.

*Intellectual Style*—In Acts 17 the apostle Paul was trying to spread the message of Jesus Christ to philosophers and the scholars of the city of Athens using an intellectual approach to evangelism. Paul was *reasoning* in the synagogues with the Jews and the God-fearing Gentiles, and in the marketplace with those who would listen. Some of the philosophers were conversing and debating with him. These philosophers needed a thinking approach that appealed to their sense of reason, and Paul was the man for the job.

*Testimonial Style*—John 9 contains a story of a blind man miraculously healed by Jesus. After his sight was restored, everybody kept asking him who healed him, saying, "Could it be the Messiah, the Son of God who healed you?" He admitted he did not have all the answers to their questions, but told them what he knew for certain: "I was blind but now I see." It was as if he said, "Draw your own conclusions. I've drawn mine; I know who it was."

This is an example of a testimonial approach to evangelism. Someone experiences a miraculous transformation through the work of Jesus Christ and then simply looks for opportunities to tell their story to others. Many people who are not very confrontational or oriented toward an intellectual approach can tell their story. They can share their testimony. They can say, "I was spiritually blind, but now I see. Christ changed my life, and He can change yours."

*Interpersonal Style*—When Matthew came to faith, he came up with the idea of throwing a party strategically designed to get his unsaved tax collector friends to rub shoulders with Jesus and the disciples. I like to call this a "party with a purpose" or a "Matthew Party." Although we all need to build relationships with those we hope to reach, those with the interpersonal approach specialize in this area by building deeper relationships with many people.

*Invitational Style*—John 4 contains the famous story of the woman at the well. After talking with Jesus at the well, this woman became convinced she had been talking to the Son of God. But rather than try to retell everything she had heard, she left her water pots and ran into the city to invite people to come and hear what Jesus had to say.

Some people are just not as articulate as others. They're not overly confident of themselves and would feel awkward explaining the Gospel to others. However, they can be very effective evangelists by simply inviting people to come hear someone else explain the Good News of Jesus. The woman at the well had a great impact because she invited many people to meet Jesus.

*Serving Style*—In Acts 9 we read about a woman named Dorcas who had an enormous impact for Christ in her community because of her habit of doing deeds of kindness. This is "service" evangelism. Through Dorcas' service to the poor and forgotten people in her city, she pointed them to the one who could forgive and transform. She may never have preached a sermon, and it's very possible she never knocked on a door or passed out literature. But she used her love and service as a vehicle to share the Gospel.

## PUTTING YOURSELF IN THE PICTURE

### BECOMING A CONTAGIOUS CHRISTIAN

I have written a book with our church's evangelism trainer, Mark Mittelberg, entitled *Becoming a Contagious Christian*. I would encourage you to get a copy and review these six evangelism styles in greater depth. These six evangelism styles are also covered in depth in another of the Interactions Bible studies, *Reaching Out: Sharing God's Love Naturally*.

### MAKING AN IMPACT LIST

Make an Impact List of the people you know who are seekers. Commit yourself to begin praying for them daily. Pray for them to grow open to the message of Jesus and for opportunities for you to show them Jesus is alive in your life. Finally, pray for the Spirit to give you courage, power, and the right words when the opportunity comes.

# WORK: TURNING DRUDGERY INTO FULFILLMENT

## REFLECTIONS FROM SESSION 4

1. If you have been reading some of the *Becoming a Contagious Christian* materials, what have you learned about evangelism that you can share with the group?
2. What have you learned about your style of evangelism and how God can use you to reach out to seekers?
3. If you have formed an Impact List with the names of seekers for whom you are praying, how has daily prayer for them impacted your attitude toward them?
4. If you have had an opportunity to talk with a seeker about your faith since the last small group meeting, tell your group members about this experience.

## THE BIG PICTURE

"I can't believe it. Now I can buy a new car, pay off my house, never work another day in my life!" Multimillion-dollar lottery winners often echo this rendition of everyone's dream. Hollywood paints the fantasy in living color each time it produces a new variation on the same old theme: Joe Average falls into enormous wealth and spends his days sipping exotic drinks on a palm-lined beach in the Caribbean. As the credits roll, we think, "That's what I'd like to do—quit work and play for the rest of my life."

Many people see work as a necessary evil. They endure the five-day workweek to support the activities of the workless weekend. They lie awake nights, scheming ways to arrange early retirement. Believing God inflicted labor on human beings as a punishment for disobedience, they imagine Him angrily screaming at Adam and Eve, "I'll fix you. From now on, you're doomed to the rock pile of human labor. The best years of your life will be wasted in work, work, work!" In their minds, work is a sentence to be served, a penance to be paid, a curse to be endured for as long as necessary. They fail to see that human labor was part of the picture *before* Adam and Eve sinned, and that the meaningful work is actually a gift of God.

## A WIDE ANGLE VIEW

**1** Take time to briefly describe to your group what you do in the course of a regular workday.

*At what points in your workday do you find joy and where do you experience stress and tension?*

## A BIBLICAL PORTRAIT

Read Colossians 3:23–24

**2** The apostle Paul says we should do all of our work for the Lord and not for men. He is clear about who we are serving when we work. In what specific ways can you serve God through what you do in the course of a workday?

## SHARPENING THE FOCUS

Read Snapshot "What Turns Your Crank?"

---

### WHAT TURNS YOUR CRANK?

 Almost all satisfied workers share one thing in common: They labor in the field of their motivated abilities. They do work consistent with their God-given abilities, talents, and interests.

Motivated abilities often appear in early childhood play. Some children have a natural aptitude for building things; in their hands simple blocks become architectural wonders. Other children find fascination in words and fill every quiet moment with books. Some spend free time on science projects. Still others gravitate naturally to athletics or the arts. Some children enjoy playing alone, while others want to invite a friend over as soon as they get home from school. Some emerge as natural leaders, while others are perfectly content to follow.

Perceptive parents can often pick up hints about possible vocational pursuits in the way their children play. Wise parents will encourage their children in those directions. It's not uncommon for satisfied workers to look back and see the seeds of their job success in their youthful recreational choices and extracurricular pursuits.

---

**3** What natural aptitudes and interests did you have as a child?

*Where do you see these interests and strengths overlapping into your present work experience?*

**4** Take a few minutes and write your ideal job description in the space provided below.

*Read your job description to your group and explain why it is ideal for you.*

*How close is this job description to what you actually do each day?*

Read Snapshot "How We Work Matters More Than We Know"

## HOW WE WORK MATTERS MORE THAN WE KNOW

We honor God by being credible workers. By striving for excellence. By earning a reputation for diligence, thoroughness, and conscientiousness. By making significant contributions to the work team.

It should never be said of Christian workers that they are halfhearted, careless, tardy, irresponsible, whiny, or negligent. Behavior like that brings reproach on God. Instead, Christian workers should epitomize character qualities like self-discipline, perseverance, and initiative. They should be self-motivated, prompt, organized, and industrious. Their efforts should result in work of the very highest quality.

Why? Because they're not just laying bricks; they're building a wall for God's glory. They're not just teaching a class; they're educating young students for God's glory. They're not just balancing the books; they're keeping the ledgers in excellent order for God's glory. They're not just driving a tractor; they're plowing a straight furrow for God's glory.

5 When a follower of Christ works with diligence and seeks excellence in all he or she does, what impact does this have on:

• other Christ followers

• seekers

• the name of Jesus

*When a follower of Christ cuts corners in the marketplace and settles for mediocrity, what impact does this have on:*

• other Christ followers

• seekers

• the name of Jesus

Read Snapshot "Setting a New Standard"

## SETTING A NEW STANDARD

In order to honor God by who we are, Christian workers need to conscientiously model a lifestyle directly opposed to the typical marketplace standard. Generally speaking, the marketplace mentality centers solely on the bottom line: profits, quotas, sales reports, balance sheets, budgets, and competition. The goal is to pump out more work in less time with lower costs. In an environment like that, people become the lowest priority.

Yet the marketplace cries out for humanness and compassion, for the touch of Christlikeness. Who can better provide that than Christian men and women who have experienced divine love and been transformed by divine power?

Yet too often Christian workers get caught up in the same self-seeking mentality that snares unbelievers. Soon they begin relegating other people to low priority status. They become robotlike in their encounters and superficial in their conversations. They no longer take time to offer compliments and affirmation, or respond to needs, or express interest in coworkers' personal lives.

Eventually coworkers get the message: "Christians are just like everybody else—more interested in profits than people; more concerned about themselves than others." It's time for Christ's followers to show the world that we are different.

**6** What are specific ways you can conduct yourself in the marketplace that would be contrary to the typical marketplace standard and show others your Christian faith is real?

Read Snapshot "What We Say Has Eternal Consequences"

## WHAT WE SAY HAS ETERNAL CONSEQUENCES

Once we earn credibility by how we work and who we are, we then become free to make an *eternal* impact in our workday world by what we *say*.

How do we start being agents of divine change, missionaries to the marketplace? We begin by praying for divinely-appointed opportunities to put our personal evangelistic styles to work. Depending on your style, that may mean going out for lunch and sharing the story of your conversion with your coworkers. Or it may mean extending mercy to a sick colleague—covering for the person at work, preparing a hot meal and delivering it at home, sending flowers or a gift of encouragement—accompanied by a simple note that says, "God has been so gracious to me. I just wanted to share some of His love with you." Or you might buy tickets to a Christian concert and offer them to coworkers, or invite them to church and to your house for Sunday brunch. You might even be led by the Spirit to confront coworkers with the futility of their pursuits and their need for a genuine encounter with Jesus Christ.

**7** Think of a seeker you are praying for right now that you have contact with through work. Picture yourself in their shoes.

*What do you plan to say or do to show them the love and care of Jesus?*

*How can your small group encourage and support you as you reach out to this person?*

**8** What are some of the rewards you experience when you do your work for the glory of God and do it with excellence?

## PUTTING YOURSELF IN THE PICTURE

### A TIME OF EVALUATION

Take time in the coming week to ask yourself the following questions:

- When I think of doing my work, how do I feel? Excited, happy, anxious, tense?
- In what ways do I see my workplace as a mission field?
- What can I do to serve God more faithfully in my workplace?
- Who is one seeker I have contact with through my work, and how can I pray for them?

### EARNING THE RIGHT TO BE HEARD

Wherever God has put you, He wants you to have an impact on those around you. If you are going to influence the seekers in your workplace with the message of Jesus, you first need to earn the right to be heard. Do your work with excellence, treat others with dignity, take time to listen, and pray for opportunities to tell others about God's love. Take time in the coming days to identify seekers in your workplace who you desire to reach with the love of Jesus. What can you do to deepen these relationships and earn the right to be heard?

# THE SEDUCTION OF MONEY

## REFLECTIONS FROM SESSION 5

1. How has your perspective on your work changed since the last time your group gathered together?
2. In what specific way can your group members be praying for you as you seek to earn the right to be heard and do evangelism in your workplace?

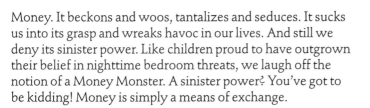 

## THE BIG PICTURE

Money. It beckons and woos, tantalizes and seduces. It sucks us into its grasp and wreaks havoc in our lives. And still we deny its sinister power. Like children proud to have outgrown their belief in nighttime bedroom threats, we laugh off the notion of a Money Monster. A sinister power? You've got to be kidding! Money is simply a means of exchange.

Meanwhile, we devote our lives to earning money, glory in spending it, and lie awake nights figuring out how to stockpile more of it. We bow at its feet and salute its command.

There's a Money Monster all right, sly and artful. What's fascinating is that as our financial needs are supplied, our appetite for money tends to increase rather than diminish. When we're physically hungry, we fill our stomachs, then back away from the table, but that's not the way it is with money. It seems the more we get, the more we want.

When I left the family business to enter the ministry, I turned down a golden opportunity for affluence. I say that with no credit to myself. I felt God's call so definitely that I simply could not refuse. For two years I ministered with no salary. Lynne taught music lessons, and we took in boarders to cover the rent. Then I began receiving thirty-five dollars a week, and then eighty-five dollars. We were thrilled!

Eventually our salary was set at twelve thousand dollars a year. I remember thinking, *Who would ever want more than twelve thousand dollars a year?* Soon I found the answer—me. As the church grew and my job description enlarged, the board of directors periodically increased my salary. Each time I thought, *Wow, this is far more than I need. Who would ever want more than this?* Twelve months later, I would find out again. Me.

Finally, I came to grips with the ugly reality that the more I had, the more I wanted. I'd been believing the Money Monster's lie that just a little bit more would be enough. But when would the drive to accumulate stop? Lynne and I decided then and there to cap my salary. The board agreed to our request, helping us strike a significant blow to the Money Monster.

## A WIDE ANGLE VIEW

1 What are some of the places the Money Monster can hide in our lives?

*How have you seen the Money Monster get a grip on your life?*

## A BIBLICAL PORTRAIT

Read 1 Timothy 6:6–10

# 2

How would you define "the love of money"?

# 3

What are some of the evils that can come when we fall in love with money and the things it can buy?

## SHARPENING THE FOCUS

Read Snapshot "Michael's Story"

### MICHAEL'S STORY

Consider Michael, a typical American child. During the most impressionable years of his life, he hears a steady stream of dinner table conversations centered almost exclusively on the things money can buy. It becomes clear to him at a young age that Mom and Dad really value money.

Over the next few years, the family moves several times because of promotions and salary increases. Michael becomes convinced that monetary increases are more important than establishing stable relational or spiritual roots.

Later on, conversations turn to college, and the dialogue focuses on what professions pay the most rather than what would best suit Michael's motivated abilities. To Michael, the apparent message is that financial remuneration will make up for lack of job fulfillment.

Michael eventually enters the job market, taking the position with the highest earning potential, yet always watching for an even better opportunity. On and on it goes, each major life decision being made on the basis of the bottom line. In time, our typical American learns to equate his self-worth with his net worth and judges others by the same standard. He eventually reaches old age, totally unaware that he's been led through life on a leash controlled by the Money Monster.

# 4

As you read the story of Michael, do you see some similarities to how you were raised? If so, how?

*What similarities and patterns from this story do you see in the way you are living your life today?*

*What are the consequences of continuing on this path?*

5 In a culture that urges us to "buy now, pay later," what drives us to play the credit game, and what are some of its potential dangers?

*What benefits can you reap if you refuse to play the credit game?*

- Financially

- Emotionally

- Relationally

- Spiritually

Read Snapshot "What's Your Central Reality?"

## WHAT'S YOUR CENTRAL REALITY?

The first step in breaking money's sinister power is to pursue a more vital relationship with Jesus Christ. People who walk with Him on a consistent, daily basis make an amazing discovery: He satisfies their soul at its deepest level. As they experience this, they find less and less need to ease the pain in their souls with the temporary anesthetics money can buy, such as expensive clothes, luxury cars, and exotic vacations.

Jesus said, "No one can serve two masters. . . . You cannot serve both God and Money" (Matt. 6:24). In other words, we cannot have two central values in our life. Either a relationship with Jesus Christ is our central value, or material gain is. We can't bow down at both altars.

**6** Why is the pursuit of a vital relationship with Jesus the only thing that will truly satisfy?

*How have you experienced this in your life?*

Read Snapshot "A Cheerful Giver"

## A CHEERFUL GIVER

I'd like to suggest a simple financial plan that almost guarantees greater financial freedom. First, pay God; second, pay yourself; third, pay the bills.

Proverbs 3:9 says, "Honor the LORD with your wealth, with the firstfruits of all your crops." That means we are to give Him the first part of our income. The Bible repeatedly suggests a minimum giving standard—a tithe—of ten percent (Matt. 23:23; Luke 11:42; Mal. 3:10). Giving a tithe allows us to express our thanksgiving for the privilege of earning wages. It also graphically demonstrates our understanding that we are not the owners of our resources; we are merely stewards of the money God has allowed us to earn.

Unfortunately, many Christians get nervous whenever they hear about tithing. They hate to do it, because it seems like a debt they'll owe for the rest of their lives, yet they feel guilty if they don't. It's a classic double bind. They wonder what ever possessed Paul to pen the words "God loves a cheerful giver" (2 Cor. 9:7).

*7* If you have made a commitment to tithing, how have you seen God provide for you and work in your life through this commitment? If you have not made that commitment, what fears or concerns are keeping you from stepping out in faith this way?

*How can a person take ten percent of what they earn, give it away, and actually be cheerful in the process?*

Read Snapshot "Save, Save, Save—How to Pay Yourself"

## SAVE, SAVE, SAVE — HOW TO PAY YOURSELF

 Eighty-five out of one hundred Americans end up with less than $250 in cash savings when they reach the age of sixty-five. During their working years they earned hundreds of thousands of dollars, but at retirement they have little to show for it. Why? Because all those years they paid everybody but themselves. Luke 10:7 says that "the worker deserves his wages," yet most people neglect their own pay.

As we've already noted, the first step to financial freedom is to pay God. The second step is to pay yourself—without apology or embarrassment. How much? That varies according to earnings and financial standings, but most financial experts recommend ten percent. The miracle of compound interest assures a sizable personal savings.

Let's say you earned fifteen thousand dollars a year for twenty-five years, and invested ten percent (thirty dollars a week) in a mutual fund at nine percent. After twenty-five years, you would have $138,500. If you earned twenty-five thousand dollars a year, you'd have $230,809!

Years ago, Lynne and I established a personal savings account that we call our "financial freedom fund." Each week, after we pay God, we pay ourselves. It's no "get-rich-quick" scheme or shortcut to financial security, but as the interest compounds, we are building a reserve of funds to be used for emergencies, education, retirement, extra giving, or whatever use God directs.

*8* Why is it so hard to put money in a savings account and leave it there?

*What would it take for you to live on eighty percent of your income?*

## PUTTING YOURSELF IN THE PICTURE

### BREAKING THE GRIP OF THE MONEY MONSTER

Take time in the coming week to identify one specific area in which the Money Monster has a grip on your life. If it is love of a material thing you own, consider giving it away. If it is an obsession of some thing or toy you feel you absolutely must have, decide not to get it. If it is a refusal to give God the first ten percent of what He puts in your care, commit yourself to tithing. Any of these actions will deal a powerful blow to the Money Monster and help you begin to experience the freedom of breaking his hold on your life.

### A COMMITMENT TO BECOME A CHEERFUL GIVER

If you have never tithed, think about what God can do through your gifts: the ministries that will be supported, the people who will be helped, the seekers who will hear the message of God's love. Pray for a cheerful and joyous heart as you give.

### LIVING ON EIGHTY PERCENT

If you feel ready for the next step, try planning so you can put some money away out of every paycheck. Ten percent is a solid figure, if you can manage it. Get some help from someone who understands investment. By saving, you will put yourself in a position where the Money Monster will have less and less control over your life. As a result, you will be freed to serve God and give generously as the Holy Spirit moves your heart to do so.

# Leader's Notes

Leading a Bible discussion—especially for the first time—can make you feel both nervous and excited. If you are nervous, realize that you are in good company. Many biblical leaders, such as Moses, Joshua, and the apostle Paul, felt nervous and inadequate to lead others (see, for example, 1 Corinthians 2:3). Yet God's grace was sufficient for them, just as it will be for you.

Some excitement is also natural. Your leadership is a gift to the others in the group. Keep in mind, however, that other group members also share responsibility for the group. Your role is simply to stimulate discussion by asking questions and encouraging people to respond. The suggestions listed below can help you to be an effective leader.

## Preparing to Lead

1. Ask God to help you understand and apply the passage to your own life. Unless that happens, you will not be prepared to lead others.
2. Carefully work through each question in the study guide. Meditate and reflect on the passage as you formulate your answers.
3. Familiarize yourself with the leader's notes for each session. These will help you understand the purpose of the session and will provide valuable information about the questions in the session.
4. Pray for the various members of the group. Ask God to use these sessions to make you better disciples of Jesus Christ.
5. Before the first session, make sure each person has a study guide. Encourage them to prepare beforehand for each session.

## Leading the Session

1. Begin the session on time. If people realize that the session begins on schedule, they will work harder to arrive on time.
2. At the beginning of your first time together, explain that these sessions are designed to be discussions, not lectures. Encourage everyone to participate, but realize some may be hesitant to speak during the first few sessions.
3. Don't be afraid of silence. People in the group may need time to think before responding.

4. Avoid answering your own questions. If necessary, rephrase a question until it is clearly understood. Even an eager group will quickly become passive and silent if they think the leader will do most of the talking.

5. Encourage more than one answer to each question. Ask, "What do the rest of you think?" or "Anyone else?" until several people have had a chance to respond.

6. Try to be affirming whenever possible. Let people know you appreciate their insights into the passage.

7. Never reject an answer. If it is clearly wrong, ask, "Which verse led you to that conclusion?" Or let the group handle the problem by asking them what they think about the question.

8. Avoid going off on tangents. If people wander off course, gently bring them back to the passage being considered.

9. Conclude your time together with conversational prayer. Ask God to help you apply those things that you learned in the session.

10. End on time. This will be easier if you control the pace of the discussion by not spending too much time on some questions or too little on others.

We encourage all small group leaders to use *Leading Life-Changing Small Groups* (Zondervan) by Bill Donahue while leading their group. Developed and used by Willow Creek Community Church, this guide is an excellent resource for training and equipping followers of Christ to effectively lead small groups. It includes valuable information on how to utilize fun and creative relationship-building exercises for your group; how to plan your meeting; how to share the leadership load by identifying, developing, and working with an "apprentice leader;" and how to find creative ways to do group prayer. In addition, the book includes material and tips on handling potential conflicts and difficult personalities, forming group covenants, inviting new members, improving listening skills, studying the Bible, and much more. Using *Leading Life-Changing Small Groups* will help you create a group that members love to be a part of.

Now let's discuss the different elements of this small group study guide and how to use them for the session portion of your group meeting.

## THE BIG PICTURE

Each session will begin with a short story or overview of the lesson theme. This is called "The Big Picture" because it introduces the central theme of the session. You will need to read this section as a group or have group members read it on their own before discussion begins. Here are three ways you can approach this section of the small group session:

- As the group leader, read this section out loud for the whole group and then move into the questions in the next section, "A Wide Angle View." (You might read the first week, but then use the other two options below to encourage group involvement.)
- Ask a group member to volunteer to read this section for the group. This allows another group member to participate. It is best to ask someone in advance to give them time to read over the section before reading it to the group. It is also good to ask someone to volunteer, and not to assign this task. Some people do not feel comfortable reading in front of a group. After a group member has read this section out loud, move into the discussion questions.
- Allow time at the beginning of the session for each person to read this section silently. If you do this, be sure to allow enough time for everyone to finish reading so they can think about what they've read and be ready for meaningful discussion.

## A WIDE ANGLE VIEW

This section includes one or more questions that move the group into a general discussion of the session topic. These questions are designed to help group members begin discussing the topic in an open and honest manner. Once the topic of the lesson has been established, move on to the Bible passage for the session.

## A BIBLICAL PORTRAIT

This portion of the session includes a Scripture reading and one or more questions that help group members see how the theme of the session is rooted and based in biblical teaching. The Scripture reading can be handled just like "The Big Picture" section: You can read it for the group, have a group member read it, or allow time for silent reading. Make sure everyone has a Bible or that you have Bibles available for those who need them. Once you have read the passage, ask the question(s) in this section so that group members can dig into the truth of the Bible.

## SHARPENING THE FOCUS

The majority of the discussion questions for the session are in this section. These questions are practical and help group members apply biblical teaching to their daily lives.

## SNAPSHOTS

The "Snapshots" in each session help prepare group members for discussion. These anecdotes give additional insight to the topic being discussed. Each "Snapshot" should be read at a designated point in the session. This is clearly marked in the session as well as in the leader's notes. Again, follow the same format as you do with "The Big Picture" section and the "Biblical Portrait" section: Either you read the anecdote, have a group member volunteer to read, or provide time for silent reading. However you approach this section, you will find these anecdotes very helpful in triggering lively dialogue and moving discussion in a meaningful direction.

## PUTTING YOURSELF IN THE PICTURE

Here's where you roll up your sleeves and put the truth into action. This portion is very practical and action-oriented. At the end of each session there will be suggestions for one or two ways group members can put what they've just learned into practice. Review the action goals at the end of each session and challenge group members to work on one or more of them in the coming week.

You will find follow-up questions for the "Putting Yourself in the Picture" section at the beginning of the next week's session. Starting with the second week, there will be time set aside at the beginning of the session to look back and talk about how you have tried to apply God's Word in your life since your last time together.

## PRAYER

You will want to open and close your small group with a time of prayer. Occasionally, there will be specific direction within a session for how you can do this. Most of the time, however, you will need to decide the best place to stop and pray. You may want to pray or have a group member volunteer to begin the lesson with a prayer. Or you might want to read "The Big Picture" and discuss the "Wide Angle View" questions before opening in prayer. In some cases, it might be best to open in prayer after you have read the Bible passage. You need to decide where you feel an opening prayer best fits for your group.

When opening in prayer, think in terms of the session theme and pray for group members (including yourself) to be responsive to the truth of Scripture and the working of the Holy Spirit. If you have seekers in your group (people investigating

Christianity but not yet believers) be sensitive to your expectations for group prayer. Seekers may not yet be ready to take part in group prayer.

Be sure to close your group with a time of prayer as well. One option is for you to pray for the entire group. Or you might allow time for group members to offer audible prayers that others can agree with in their hearts. Another approach would be to allow a time of silence for one-on-one prayers with God and then to close this time with a simple "Amen."

# A New Dimension in Spirituality

## PSALM 46

### INTRODUCTION

Some years ago I got tired of the daily descent into inauthentic Christianity. I decided then to either do something to stop it, or to get out of the ministry. Christendom didn't need another inauthentic leader.

I began to pray for guidance and to experiment with various disciplines that would help me be more consistent. Eventually I developed a three-phased discipline that I employ every day to keep me truly "connected" to God. It's not the only path to spiritual authenticity, but for me and many of my friends, coworkers, and church members, it's proven to be a genuinely life-changing discipline.

The steps are fairly simple. First, I spend time journaling and reflecting on yesterday. Through this, I seek to live an examined and reflective life. Second, I pray using a simple four-step prayer (adoration, confession, thanksgiving, and supplication). And third, I seek to quiet my heart and listen to God. In this session you will walk through these three steps with your small group and discover how you can grow in your prayer life and become authentic in your relationship with God.

### THE BIG PICTURE

Take time to read this introduction with the group. There are suggestions for how this can be done in the beginning of this leader's section.

### A WIDE ANGLE VIEW

**Question One** In the introduction I gave an example of how easy it is to slide into inauthentic Christian living. It can happen in the first half hour of our day. It can happen in our marriages, parenting, work, faith, friendships, and every other area of life. If we are going to move away from these patterns of inauthentic living and move toward fully authentic lives, we need to first identify what inauthenticity looks like in ourselves and others. Allow group members to openly discuss some of their own patterns and areas of struggle.

## A BIBLICAL PORTRAIT
**Read Psalm 46**

## SHARPENING THE FOCUS
### Read Snapshot "Put It in Writing" before Question 3

**Question Three** My first journal entry said this: "Yesterday I said I hated the concept of journals, and I still do. But if this is what it takes to rid myself of inauthentic spirituality, I'll do it. If this is what it takes to reduce my RPMs enough to talk and walk with Christ, I'll do it. I'll journal."

The truth is, I have been journaling almost every day since then. I've never written anything profound, but in simple terms I've chronicled the activity of God in my life, relationships, marriage, children, and ministry. I've also worked through feelings, confronted fears, and weighed decisions. And I've slowed down enough to meet with God.

### Read Snapshot "Yesterday" before Question 4

**Question Four** As the group leader, encourage each person to take about five minutes to try journaling. There is space provided in the session. Some will find this process very easy and natural; others might struggle to put something on paper. The goal is not to get everyone to fill up the space on the page, but to reflect honestly on their day. Journaling is about being reflective and honest before God.

Let group members know you will not be asking them to read any of their journaling to the group. These are private moments of self-examination.

The question of what someone learned through this brief journaling experience can be answered in a least two different ways. Some might respond by telling about something they learned while they analyzed their previous day. Others could respond by telling about what they learned about themselves through the process of journaling. Invite responses on both levels.

### Read Snapshot "Now What?" before Question 5

**Question Five** As I look back on my growth in prayer, I realize I always had good intentions. I *tried* to pray. But I would get down on my knees and say, "Dear God . . ." and in five seconds my mind would be in outer space. I would start thinking of people I hadn't seen in years, making up solutions for problems that didn't exist, strategizing for new ministries, or planning family vacations.

It was so frustrating. I normally have tremendous ability to concentrate. I pride myself on being able to stick with a project until it's done. But prayer did me in every time. I would hear people speak of praying for four hours, and I would feel terrible knowing I couldn't pray for four minutes.

I would probably still be a prayerless man if a friend hadn't suggested his habit of writing out his prayers. He said God created him with a very active mind, and the only way he had been able to "capture" it and focus on God was to write out his prayers. I thought, "That's me! That's what I need to do."

Another concern I had about my prayer life was imbalance. I knew how easy it was to fall into the "Please God" syndrome. "Please God, give me . . . help me . . . comfort me . . . strengthen me." I didn't want to do that. I wanted to pray with balance. So I adopted a simple pattern of talking to God that's not original with me. It includes the following four sturdy legs of balanced prayer.

*Adoration*—Though I've been a Christian for years, I never privately worshiped God on a consistent basis—until I started writing out my prayers. Worship is foreign to us. Because of sin, worship doesn't come naturally. We have to work at it; we have to be disciplined about it. And like any other learned activity, the first few times we try it, we feel awkward. But we need to remember that our sincerity, not our eloquence, is what matters to God.

There are several reasons for beginning prayer with worship and adoration. First, worship reminds us that we're addressing the Holy Majestic God and prevents us from reducing prayer to a wish list—the "Please God" syndrome again.

Second, worship reestablishes the identity of God. It reminds us that God has power to intervene in any situation, that He cares about us, and that whether we're in a car, an office, or on an airplane, He is always available to us.

Adoration also purges. After five or ten minutes in adoration, I find my spirit has been softened, my heart purified. My agenda changes. That burning issue I just *had* to bring to God's attention suddenly seems less crucial. My sense of desperation subsides. I begin to say, and mean, "It is well with my soul. I am enjoying You, God. I am at peace."

Finally, adoration is the appropriate introduction to prayer simply because God deserves it.

Begin to worship God when you pray. Be creative. Experiment. Use choruses and psalms to get you started. Don't worry if you feel clumsy at first. God's heart is thrilled by even our most feeble attempts.

*Confession*—I used to be an "oops" confessor. I would say an unkind word to someone, then say, "Oops, Lord, I'll have to confess that to You later." Then I would exaggerate a story, and say, "Oops, Lord, I'll catch that one later too." All day I would add to the tally, fully intending to clear the bill later.

But later seldom came. When it did, I would make a blanket confession of "my many sins." I thought I was being wonderfully honest and humble to claim my sins like that. In reality, it was a colossal cop-out.

You see, blanket confessions are virtually painless, but they do nothing to transform our hearts. It seems confession has to hurt a bit, even embarrass us, before we'll take it seriously. That is why writing out our confessions and seeing those words on paper can be such a powerful experience.

In one particular Sunday message, I emphasized the fact that we're all sinners who need a Savior. After the service, a salesman informed me that he didn't consider himself a sinner. I asked if he'd been absolutely faithful to his wife. "Well, I travel a lot, you know. . . ." Then I asked about his expense account. "Oh, everybody stretches the truth a bit. . . ." Finally, I questioned his sales techniques. Did he ever exaggerate or overstate a claim? "That's standard in the industry. . . ."

"Well," I said, "you've just told me you're an adulterer, a cheater, and a liar." "How dare you call me those awful things!" he huffed. He was appalled by what he called my "brash insensitivity."

As hard as it was for that man to hear those words, I believe I did him a favor. I also believe I do myself a favor when I write in my journal "I am a liar. I am greedy. I have a problem with lust. I am envious."

Two things happen when we confess our sins honestly. First, we experience the freedom of forgiveness. For years I tried to run the race of faith with chains of unconfessed sin tangled around my legs. I didn't know how much my sins were hindering me until I quit playing games and got honest with God.

Second, gratitude for God's forgiveness motivates us to forsake our sin. Why hurt Someone who loves us that much? Why disobey Someone who extends grace to us?

There doesn't appear to be much true confession in Christian circles. That's a shame, because exciting things happen when God's children get honest about their sin. Five days of having to call oneself a liar, a greedy person, or a cheat is enough to drive any spiritually sensitive person to forsake that sin.

We all have to realize that sin is serious business and that we need to enlist the Holy Spirit's help in forsaking it. Only then can we make progress in rooting specific sins out of our lives and know what Scripture means when it says, "the old has gone, the new has come!" (2 Cor. 5:17).

*Thanksgiving*—Do you remember the ten lepers described in Luke 17? They begged Jesus to heal them, but when He did, only one of them bothered to thank Him. Jesus asked, "Where are the other nine?"

I am confident that the other nine were thankful. They had to be. If you had a debilitating, terminal illness that rotted your limbs and made you a social outcast, and suddenly you were cleansed and healed, wouldn't you have tremendous feelings of gratitude toward your Healer? Of course you would. But nine lepers didn't take the time to say it. And that mattered to Jesus.

One summer I took my son, Todd, for a helicopter ride at a county fair. He was so excited he could hardly stand it. Later, I thought he was asleep in the car until he slid his arm around my shoulder and said, "Dad, I just want to thank you for taking me to that fair." That expression of gratitude tempted me to turn the car around and go back for round two.

When I understood the distinction between feeling gratitude and expressing thanksgiving, I decided to become a more "thanks-giving" man. I want to be like the one leper who ran back and showered Jesus with thanks. I want to be like Todd, who warmed my heart with his gratitude.

An added benefit of giving thanks is a transformed attitude. I used to be a very covetous man. I struggled hard with wanting more than I had. But a daily look at my blessings has led me from covetousness to contentment to awe at the abundance in my life.

*Supplication*—"Do not be anxious about anything, but in every-thing, by prayer and petition, with thanksgiving, present your requests to God" (Phil. 4:6). After adoring God, confessing our sins, and thanking Him for His goodness, we're in the right frame of mind to ask God for what we need.

Nothing is too big for God to handle or too small for Him to be interested in. But sometimes I still wonder if my requests are legitimate. So I'm honest with God. I say, "God, I've told You how I feel about this situation. You've asked me to make my requests known, so I have. I would love to see You do this. But if You have other plans, I don't want to get in the way. If these requests are wrong, or the timing isn't right, that's fine. We'll go Your way."

Sometimes I don't even know how to begin to pray about a certain situation. Then I say, "I don't know what to say, Lord. If You'll tell me how to pray, I'll pray that way."

God honors that kind of prayer. James 1:5 says, "If any of you lacks wisdom, he should ask God, who gives generously to all without finding fault, and it will be given to him."

### Read Snapshot "Listening" before Question 6

**Question Six** Allow five to ten minutes for silence and listening. It might be helpful, if possible, to allow your group members to move to different areas of the room in which you are gathered. Invite them to silently seek God and ask the questions listed in the above Snapshot. Also, encourage them to write down any answered prayers or impressions they receive during this time of listening prayer. Let them know you will tell the group when it is time to gather together again.

In my own devotional time, I approach this time of listening by first asking, "What is the next step in my relationship with You?" Sometimes I sense nothing, and interpret that to mean, "We're all right. Don't worry. If I wanted to say something I would. Just relax in My presence."

At other times God seems to say, "Just trust Me. I'll help you." Often God leads me to do things I'm uncertain of, and it's easy to start operating out of fear. That's when He reminds me that He's trustworthy. He'll be strong in my weakness; He'll be adequate in my inadequacy.

Other times He tells me I need to learn more about His character. One time I sensed God telling me to loosen up. I was too concerned about trying to please Him, and had to learn to enjoy Him more.

Second, I ask, "What's the next step in the development of my character?" I always get a response from this one. There

seems to be plenty of rough edges for God to chip away at!
"Honesty," He'll say, or "humility" or "purity."

God has taught me that, in regard to character, little things
matter. At the office, I usually do only ministry-related correspondence; the church pays the postage. Occasionally,
however, the distinction between ministry and personal correspondence blurs. Once during my listening time, I sensed
God telling me to be more scrupulous in distinguishing between
ministry and personal mail. That afternoon I taped quarters to
two of my outgoing letters. My secretary said, "What's this?"
I said, "Just pay the meter. It's important." It's such a little
thing. But not to God.

Third, I ask, "What's the next step in my family life?" Again,
God gets specific. "Be more encouraging to Lynne. Take time
to serve her." Or, "You've been out of town a lot. Plan a special
getaway with the kids." Being a godly husband and father is a
tremendous challenge for me. I need God's suggestions.

Finally, I ask, "What's the next step in my ministry?" I don't
know how anyone survives ministry without listening to
God. Most of my ideas for illustrations, messages, and new
ministry directions come out of this time of listening. I would
have little creativity and insight without it.

The great adventure of listening to God can be scary sometimes.
Often God tells me to call or write to someone, or apologize
for something I've done, or give away a possession, or start a
new ministry, and I think, *Why? I don't understand.*

But I'm learning to walk more and more by faith. God's lead-
ings don't have to make sense. Some of the wisest direction
I've received has seemed ridiculous from a human viewpoint.

So if God tells you to write someone, write. If He tells you to
serve somewhere, serve. Trust Him, and take the risk.

## PUTTING YOURSELF IN THE PICTURE

Let the group members know you will be providing time at
the beginning of the next meeting for them to discuss how
they have put their faith into action. Let them tell about how
they have acted on one of the two options listed in this section.
However, don't limit their interaction to these two options.
They may have put themselves into the picture in some other
way as a result of your session. Allow for honest and open
communication.

Also, be clear that there will not be any kind of a "test" or forced reporting. All you are going to do is allow time for people to volunteer to talk about how they have applied what they learned in your last study. Some group members will feel pressured if they think you are going to make everyone report on how they acted on these action goals. You don't want anyone to skip the next session because they are afraid of having to say they did not follow up on what they learned from the prior lesson. The key is to provide a place for honest communication without creating pressure and fear of being embarrassed.

Every session from this point on will open with a look back at the "Putting Yourself in the Picture" section of the previous session.

# TRUTH-TELLING: THE PATHWAY TO AUTHENTIC RELATIONSHIPS
## EPHESIANS 4:14–16, 25

### INTRODUCTION

Honesty is essential for authentic relationships. This is true of friendships, marriages, work relationships, and every other kind of relationship. Too often we buy the lie that "making peace" is better than telling the truth. From our childhood, we are taught to "shake hands, apologize, and make up." Too often this process is an effort to solve a problem without ever addressing what it is. For too long we have "buried the hatchet" by trying to pretend everything is fine, when the truth is, there are still battle scars that need to be healed.

This interaction is about the tough but necessary practice of telling the truth, even when it hurts. In this session we will discover how to enter the tunnel of turmoil and come out on the other side with better and more authentic relationships.

### THE BIG PICTURE

Take time to read this introduction with the group. There are suggestions for how this can be done in the beginning of this leader's section.

### A BIBLICAL PORTRAIT

**Read Ephesians 4:14–16, 25**

### SHARPENING THE FOCUS

**Read Snapshot "A Great Theory, but ..."
before Question 3**

**Question Three** One day when I was getting ready to step out of the shower at the YMCA where I work out, I noticed another man step out ahead of me. After making sure no one was watching, he grabbed *my* towel, dried himself, threw the towel on the floor, and then headed for the locker room. I couldn't believe it!

I was upset by his action, and being the forthright, fearless, outspoken, born activist that I am . . . I said absolutely nothing. I've learned over the years to mind my manners around people bigger and stronger than I. But this guy was little and old and still I said nothing—on the outside. On the inside, however, I was raging. "Excuse me, mister. That was my towel you just profaned. And I am more than a little perturbed about it!"

The man didn't know it was my towel he had just ripped off, so when I entered the locker room, he tried to engage me in friendly conversation about the stock market, the Chicago Bears, the weekend, the weather forecast. What did I do? I submerged my feelings about what he had done and joined in the conversation. We dressed and parted ways.

But do you know what? The next time I see that man, the first thought that's going to cross my mind is, *Why did he swipe my towel?* That man doesn't know it, but there's a major blockage in our relationship.

I could've said, "Excuse me, sir, that's my towel" or "Sir, did you forget your towel? I'll be happy to get you one." Why didn't I engage myself in the situation honestly? I'll tell you why. Because it's human nature to prefer peacekeeping over truth-telling. Most of us will do almost anything to avoid conflict.

Years ago I saw a television show where a camera was hidden in a restaurant. An actor entered, sat next to a man eating at the counter, and without saying a word, grabbed some french fries off the man's plate. This scenario was repeated numerous times, and nine times out of ten the victims never said a word. You knew they were doing a slow burn inside; they clenched their fists and glared at the thief in disbelief. But they never said a word.

When people submerge their true feelings in order to preserve harmony, they undermine the integrity of a relationship. They buy peace on the surface, but underneath there are hurt feelings, troubling questions, and hidden hostilities just waiting to erupt. It's a costly price to pay for a cheap peace that inevitably leads to inauthentic relationships.

### Read Snapshot "Enter the Tunnel" before Question 4

**Questions Four & Five** Awful things can happen in the tunnel of chaos. One person in a relationship may decide to leave the counterfeit peace of pseudocommunity by revealing a long-concealed wound that hampers the relationship. Timidly, he enters the tunnel. It's scary, but he cares about the relationship and wants to improve it. So he takes the risk.

What happens? The counterfeit peace shatters in an explosion of hostility that feels terrible.

I know.

Early in our marriage I realized that Lynne and I were in pseudocommunity. I didn't know the term back then, but I knew I felt detached from Lynne because of grievances I had stored up against her. I'm a fairly confrontational person, and I decided to air these issues so I could relate to Lynne more authentically.

During a vacation at a beautiful lake in Wisconsin, I asked her to join me on the dock. It was a lovely evening; the water shimmered in the golden glow of the sinking sun. It was the perfect time for a little heart-to-heart talk. I carefully articulated the truth as I saw it. My communication skills left a bit to be desired, but I spoke as lovingly and sensitively as I knew how to at that time. I fully expected a comfortable conversation and a heartfelt apology.

Instead I watched as my beautiful, spiritual, well-mannered, five-foot-four, one-hundred-and-five-pound French poodle turned into a Doberman pinscher. With both ears laid back, her eyes on fire, and her teeth bared, she let me have it! I couldn't believe it.

I decided then and there that truth-telling was a bad idea. Maybe pseudocommunity wasn't ideal, but it sure beat chaos. I wanted my French poodle back! I decided to opt for Plan B: submerge my feelings; suppress the truth; ignore the issues; back off; keep the peace.

In all fairness to Lynne, I have to tell you that her attempts at truth-telling had met with the same resistance. More than once in the early years of our marriage, she tried to tell me how deeply my workaholism was wounding her. More than once, I stonewalled her, suggesting that she fix her insecurities, grow up, and "help me instead of hold me back."

Eventually, she too settled for Plan B.

What did we accomplish? We simply postponed our appointment in the tunnel. We thought that if we ignored our problems they would eventually go away. Instead, they turned over and over in our minds, like meat on a rotisserie grill, and became more and more inflamed. The chaos we eventually faced made that evening on the dock look like child's play.

We each made the mistake of believing that the other's initial defensiveness was the end of the world, so we backed off. In reality, the defensive reaction was simply the opening to the tunnel of chaos. If we had entered the tunnel and then talked our problems through to a resolution, we could have moved into true community. But we were so frightened, we made a U-turn and headed back into years of pseudocommunity.

Thank God, our frustration eventually led us to tell the truth and let the chips fall. We did find out that the tunnel of chaos is a frightening place to be. But when we came out the other side, we realized that going through the tunnel was a small price to pay for the open communication and freed-up love of an authentic relationship. It was worth it.

**Read Snapshot "Have You Seen This Person?" before Question 6**

**Question Six** For the purposes of providing background information, I have further developed some of these characters who don't want to pay the price for open communication. Oh, they're all for authentic relationships. They desperately want to enjoy true community with family and friends. But they're convinced they can get there without going through the tunnel. They know how traumatic truth-telling can be, so they've come up with some "safer" methods.

*Henry the Hintdropper*—Henry believes outright truth-telling is crude, brash, and upsetting, so he devises an ingenious plan to accomplish the same objective, without actually having to tell the truth.

Henry has been in pseudocommunity with his wife since she decided to reenter the marketplace. She's having a hard time juggling a full-time job, two junior high kids, a husband, a house, and meals, and Henry is having a hard time adjusting to her new schedule. He's feeling a bit neglected by his once-attentive wife. At first he tries to submerge his frustration and not say anything, but eventually detachment and bitterness set in. He decides he has to do something. He wants to move out of pretense and back into marital intimacy where he belongs.

He could say, "Honey, I'm hurt. I feel neglected. I know you're juggling a lot, but we can't go on like this. How can I help? What solution can we come up with?"

But that's not Henry's style.

Instead, one night as his wife scrambles to get dinner on the table, Henry looks over the top of his *Wall Street Journal* and says, "You know, honey, I'm thinking of buying stock in Stouffer's frozen dinners." *Oh, that was a good one,* he thinks to himself. She says, "What did you mean by that, Henry?" He says, "Oh, nothing. I just heard some takeover rumors." He only wants to plant a seed, you know.

Later that evening Henry tells his wife that a friend at work finds romantic notes tucked in his pocket three times a week. "That's some woman Frank's married to." He thinks he's really communicating now. He's on a roll! The capper comes when he tells his wife he saw an ad for a new outfit called "Rent-a-Wife."

While Henry congratulates himself on his clever subtlety, his wife contemplates the joys of homicide. Eventually she says, "Okay, Henry, cut the games. Enough cute stuff. If you have a problem, let's talk about it!" She doesn't appreciate his hint-dropping ploys, and in an instant, they're smack dab in the middle of the tunnel.

Hint-droppers may want to avoid the tunnel at all costs, but they only postpone the meeting. In the process, they add insult to injury by heaping all the damage done during the hint-dropping era on top of the initial problem.

*Mary the Manipulator*—Mary has a serious marriage problem: her husband. He's a mild-mannered, peace-loving, laid-back man who's not nearly as motivated or energetic as Mary thinks he should be. And she should know, shouldn't she? I mean, isn't *she* the standard by which everyone else is to be evaluated?

After six years of marriage to a man who uses only sixty-watt lightbulbs, she's had it. It's time to do something—to "should" him into action. "Carl, you should do something. Every time I see you, you're vegetating." "Carl, you should spend more time with Jimmy. He's having trouble with math again." "Carl, you should take night classes and improve yourself." "Carl, you shouldn't spend so much time watching TV." "Carl, you should take up jogging." She's like a recording: Carl, you should. Carl, you shouldn't.

Mary hopes to reshape Carl into someone with whom she can experience true community. Little does she know what's going on in Carl's head while he lies on the couch listening to her rantings. He's marveling at her arrogance and moralizing. He's astounded by her not-so-well-concealed attempts to recreate him. This mild-mannered man is on the brink of coming to life!

He's about to stand up and say, "Okay, Mary, enough is enough. I'm different from you, Mary—no better or no worse, just different. God made me this way, and you have no right to try to remake me in your image. If you would like me to take up jogging, then feel free to tell me that. You have a right to express your desires. But don't tell me I *should* do it. Only God can tell me what I should and should not do. Understand?"

Mary wanted to avoid the tunnel, but she's in it now! And Carl's hoppin' mad about her manipulating ways. Her "safer method" got her in deep weeds.

*Gary the Guilt-tripper*—Gary's trump card is one we're all familiar with. "Gee, Fred! After *all* I've done for you, you refuse to do this one little thing for me. How *could* you?" Or, "Jim, what do you mean, you can't go with me! I was *depending* on you. Now I'll have to go alone, and I'll probably get mugged or something!" Or, "Well, if *that's* all your mother and I mean to you . . . okay then . . . you'll get no complaint from us." Or, as I heard recently, "It's your choice, Pastor Hybels. If you won't respond to my request, I'll go to a church where the pastor *loves* his people. There's no reason to stay at *this* church!"

Don't you just love being spoken to like that? Nothing brings out the worst in us like a good, old-fashioned guilt trip. The guilt-tripper's goal is to get what he wants, and often he does, but always at the expense of authenticity. People may give in to the guilt-tripper's demands, but the wheels of rebellion are set in motion, and the ultimate destination is the tunnel of chaos.

*Ivan the Intimidator*—Ivan gets really upset when his feelings get hurt. He's not content just to talk about it; he wants to "blow somebody away." He intimidates other people into submission. Ivan spends half his life in the tunnel and doesn't even know it.

*More Not-So-Notable Characters*—Steve the Stonewaller gets hurt, pouts, slams doors, shuffles around with his head down, and groans instead of breathes. Sooner or later people notice the commotion and express concern: "Hey, Steve, do we have a problem? Is there something you want to talk about?" Steve says, "We don't have a problem. And if we do, I *don't* want to talk about it." How's that for truth-telling?

Steve's sister, Sarah, plays the same game from a slightly different position. "Is something wrong, Sarah?" "No," she whimpers. "Are you sure?" She nods an unconvincing "yes." You walk away to the sound of her woeful sighs.

**Read Snapshot "Guidelines for Truth-telling" before Question 7**

**Question Eight** A man in my church gave me permission to quote the following letter.

> Dear Bill:
>
> My company's vice president is in the habit of riding roughshod over me, and I've developed the habit of swallowing my feelings about it. Well, today my boss did it again. This time I gave my reaction to the Lord, and the Lord produced flashbacks of some of your recent messages on truth-telling.
>
> I decided not to submerge my anger any longer. I walked into my boss's office, trusting the Lord for the right words to say. The resulting conversation was refreshingly honest—and a breakthrough for me and my employer. How thankful I am for God's plan of telling the truth.

That man said, "Enough is enough. I've had it with pseudo-community." He walked into the tunnel trusting God, played no games, and came out the other side on the path to a relational authenticity.

Just for a moment, think of the key people in your life—spouse, children, parents, friends, neighbors, coworkers. Ask yourself two questions about your relationship with them. Are you telling the truth to these people? Or are you in pseudocommunity, where the basic value is peacekeeping at any cost?

Chances are, some or many of those relationships are pseudo-relationships. They're blocked by grievances or concerns you're afraid to talk about because you know a confrontation will force you into the tunnel of chaos.

If that's true, please remember this: The counterfeit peace of inauthentic relationships always deteriorates into relational death. Therefore, you *must* pursue truth-telling; you *must* risk the tunnel. Walk into it and wrestle with the truth. Use careful, honest forms of communication, and then trust God to bring you out the other side. As unpleasant as it seems, entering this tunnel is the first major step toward relational authenticity.

## PUTTING YOURSELF IN THE PICTURE

Challenge group members to take time in the coming week to use part or all of this application section as an opportunity for continued growth.

## A CLOSING NOTE

I would like to end this session here, but integrity demands I add one more point. Sometimes deception runs so deep in a relationship that temporary suspension of the relationship may be necessary. This is particularly true when there is substance abuse (drugs or alcohol), emotional or physical abuse, immorality, financial deception, or spiritual hypocrisy. If long-term, consistent truth-telling fails to result in relational healing, there may be no acceptable alternative. If this is the case with one of your group members, work with a Christian counselor or a church pastor to help navigate through this process.

A young woman in my church had suffered extreme child abuse at the hands of her parents. Her counselor encouraged her to talk with her parents about it to open the way for personal healing and relational authenticity. Repeatedly her parents denied any wrongdoing and accused her of trying to destroy their lives and reputation. Their deception so traumatized her and thwarted her healing process that her counselor recommended a temporary suspension of all attempts to relate to them.

Occasionally our church counselors recommend that spouses of alcoholics temporarily suspend their relationship with their husband or wife. Deception is often so ingrained in alcoholics' thought processes that honest communication is absolutely impossible. Only detoxification can free them to relate authentically. It often takes the dramatic suspension of a significant relationship to force them to get the help they need.

If you're trapped in a relationship so steeped in deception that honest communication seems impossible, seek the counsel of godly people. With their help, determine the course of action that will best serve both you and the other person. If temporary suspension of the relationship is necessary, pray that God will use it to shatter the deception and open the way for future reconciliation.

# HONEST EMOTIONS

## 2 CORINTHIANS 4:7–12

### INTRODUCTION

If we are going to be authentic followers of Christ, it is essential for us to surrender our whole lives to Him. This includes our emotions. Too often we keep our feelings and emotions to ourselves and try to live with hurt and anger bottled up deep in our hearts. God wants to offer healing and wholeness, but this can come only when we acknowledge our pain to ourselves, God, and others.

In this session we will be challenged to be honest with God about our emotions. We will see how this will lead to healing and wholeness that we can never experience if we live inauthentically, denying the pain and hurt in our lives.

Because this is such a tender topic, enter this session prayerfully and with great sensitivity. If you discover a group member who lives with pain and struggles that are deeply rooted in their past, you may want to encourage them to meet with a pastor or to pursue Christian counseling as part of the healing process.

### THE BIG PICTURE

Take time to read this introduction with the group. There are suggestions for how this can be done in the beginning of this leader's section.

### A BIBLICAL PORTRAIT

**Read 2 Corinthians 4:7–12**

**Question Two** Paul applied this principle repeatedly. He wrote to the Corinthian church, "We are hard pressed on every side, but not crushed; perplexed, but not in despair; persecuted, but not abandoned; struck down, but not destroyed. We always carry around in our body the death of Jesus, so that the life of Jesus may also be revealed in our body" (2 Cor. 4:8–10).

Paul acknowledged the dreadful reality of living in a sin-stained, evil-tarnished world. But true to form, he looked beyond the pain to something he could rejoice in. There may be pain, he said, but it will neither crush us nor throw us into despair; we'll be neither abandoned nor destroyed.

Why? Because "we know that the one who raised the Lord Jesus from the dead will also raise us with Jesus and present us with you in his presence" (2 Cor. 4:14). In the fiercest storms and the darkest nights, when there's not one iota of temporal comfort to cling to, Paul rejoices in the eternal reality of heaven. The day is coming when the same power that raised Jesus from the dead is going to raise us to life eternal!

## SHARPENING THE FOCUS

**Read Snapshot "Rejoice! Rejoice! Rejoice!"
before Question 3**

**Question Three** Paul says, "Rejoice in the Lord always; and if you have any confusion about that, let me say it again, rejoice!" Many Christians decide to rejoice no matter what— even if that means denying their pain, loss, anger, embarrassment, hurt, or feelings of abandonment. Even if they have to bury their unfinished business one more time. They've been taught that the Christian cure for grief is to spiritualize it away. If they praise God passionately enough, the full effect of the tragedy will never take hold. It's like a Teflon shield. Just pray, and the grief will slide right off.

Some Christians make heroes of people who smile and sing their way through funerals of loved ones. They make role models of those who never crack, never cry, never stop praising God in the midst of the deepest valleys. If only other Christians would be like them. If they would just listen to more messages, memorize more verses, and fill their minds with more Christian music, they too could submerge the pain and "Praise the Lord anyway!"

But in your heart of hearts, don't you sometimes wonder? Is all that rejoicing real? Or does denial play a role? Are valid emotions being submerged? Are pain and anger and hurt being stuffed into a vault that's going to explode someday?

I have actually heard sincere, godly women say things like this: "Bill, just last night I found out that my husband's been unfaithful. But it's okay. I'm sure God has a better plan. He's going to work this out. My husband may not be faithful, but God is. With your help, the elders' prayers, and my friends' support, I'm going to be fine."

Such a controlled response in a situation like that makes me uneasy. I wanted to shake her and say, "Dear friend, it's all right for you to be so mad right now that you can't talk straight. It's all right for you to feel so violated you want to fall in a pile and cry until someone picks you up. It's okay to admit those feelings." I get very uncomfortable when Christians try to prove their maturity and love for God by refusing to acknowledge legitimate pain. I fear they're not being authentic in regard to their emotions.

**Read Snapshot "Suffer, Suffer, Suffer!" before Question 4**

**Question Four** As people abandon their faith in God, they plummet into the abyss of personal agony and eventually become sickened with self-pity and hopelessness. They take their eyes off Christ, stop reading the Bible, stop praying, and stop listening to the encouragement of Christian friends. They isolate themselves from all avenues of divine intervention and slide into utter despair. In the end, they quietly whisper, "Where's God in all this? Does He have *no* role to play in my attempt to cope? Must I face the rogue winds of life all alone?"

Philippians 4:4 obviously decries such an approach. But I believe the spirit of the verse also decries the first approach. The kind of rejoicing Paul spoke of requires no overspiritual-ized denial of emotional authenticity. His "rejoicing" requires a rugged, mature faith that authentically acknowledges both the pains of life and the power of God.

**Question Five** Paul teaches us that it is possible to "rejoice in the Lord" even when we are facing painful situations. This does not mean we should thank God for pain, suffering, or evil. However, we *can* find where God is working through our situation and rejoice in the good God brings—even from painful experiences.

The first chapter of Philippians gives a glimpse into the context from which Paul admonished his readers to rejoice. To begin with, he was in prison. What made that especially distressing was that something terrible was happening outside his locked cell. Hucksters were on the circuit, preaching Christ with impure motives and taking up offerings to fill their own pockets.

It was unthinkable to Paul that people use the Gospel of Christ to elevate themselves and build personal empires. Besides, it was unfair. Evil men were free to preach, while Paul, who loved the Lord sincerely, was locked in a prison cell.

Certainly Paul had little reason to rejoice. And he *didn't* rejoice—at least not about being in prison or about evil men "using" the message of Christ. But read what he wrote in Philippians 1:18: "But what does it matter? The important thing is that in every way, whether from false motives or true, Christ is preached. And because of this I rejoice." What did he rejoice in? That Christ was being preached.

He didn't gloss over the issue of hucksters. He didn't try to convince the readers of his letter that everything in Philippi was just fine. He said, "There's something rotten going on here, and it distresses me deeply." But he didn't dwell on the damage being done by the hucksters or drown himself and others in seas of despair. He didn't say, "The church in Philippi is doomed. We might as well close up shop and go home."

Paul acknowledged the hucksters, openly lamented their threat, and then placed the whole tragedy in the context of God's overall activity in the world. That freed him to rejoice in the one little part of the whole fiasco that was indeed praiseworthy— that even if it was done for wrong motives, at least Christ was being preached. In that, Paul could genuinely rejoice.

Philippians 2:14–18 provides another illustration of Paul's style of rejoicing. In this passage Paul challenges his readers to "become blameless and pure, children of God without fault in a crooked and depraved generation" (v. 15). Why did he want them to do this? So that "I may boast on the day of Christ that I did not run or labor for nothing" (v. 16). Paul wanted them to remain steadfast in their faith so he could rejoice in two things: First, that his efforts to establish and nurture that little group of believers had lead to genuinely transformed lives; and second, that someday he would receive a reward from the Lord for his faithful service.

He continued with these words: "Even if I am being poured out like a drink offering on the sacrifice and service coming from your faith, I am glad and rejoice" (v. 17). In the midst of beatings, imprisonment, and impending death there was something Paul could sincerely rejoice in.

Paul didn't deny the reality of the situation; he openly acknowledged that he was sitting on death row, "being poured out like a drink offering." But he didn't drown in self-pity because of that. He found something in that ugly situation worth rejoicing about: that lives had been changed and someday he would be rewarded for his part in that process. That's what he chose to focus on.

Paul gives a final, simple challenge to his Philippian readers to "Rejoice in the Lord always. I will say it again: Rejoice!"

(Phil. 4:4). In other words, "Do what I did. Whatever situation you're in, find something praiseworthy. Don't deny the problems. Don't ignore the hurt. But find some little part of the situation that's praiseworthy, and in that you can 'rejoice in the Lord always.'"

### Read Snapshot "So What Do We Do Now?" before Question 6

**Question Six** Allow about five minutes for personal time of reflection and writing. You may want to allow group members to move to different parts of the room for this exercise.

**Question Seven** Allow about five minutes for group members to pray silently and express their hearts to God.

**Question Eight** *Refuse to deny the pain*—Sure, it's hard to give up our Norman Rockwell picture of life, but that's not reality. Reality is that our parents were imperfect and behaved in ways that brought us pain. Reality is that miscarriages cause grief. Reality is that wayward teenagers can rip a parent's heart out. Reality is that losing a job can create feelings of fear and anxiety. Reality is that sexual abuse causes devastation. Reality is that there is heartache in this world, and sometimes you and I are caught in the middle of it.

When that's true, we need to acknowledge our gut-level responses: We need to admit to ourselves that we're afraid, lonely, disappointed, or angry.

*Honestly tell God how you feel*—Being honest to God was a hard thing for me to grasp because my religious background placed tremendous emphasis on God's transcendence. I heard over and over again that God was sovereign and holy. While that is true, it was so overemphasized that it led to a deterministic theology that said, in effect, "God decreed it, so don't ask questions. Just be quiet and go along with the program."

Then I started reading the Bible on my own and was totally tripped up by the Psalms. Repeatedly, David expressed his heartfelt confusion: "God, I don't understand this. How can You treat me this way? How can You allow this? Why do the righteous suffer while the wicked prosper? Help me understand this!" David, "a man after God's own heart," certainly didn't have a "God-decreed-it-so-don't-ask-questions" mindset (see Ps. 73).

What I've learned is that often these authentic outpourings of frustration, or even anger, are necessary steps on the path to wholeness. The cathartic process of pouring our hearts out to the Lord, of emptying ourselves of pent-up emotions and unanswered questions, opens the way for insight and understanding.

The same thing happens to us that so often happened to the psalmist. After the outburst comes the renewed perspective. The lights go on. We realize anew that, in spite of the heartache or the unanswered questions, God is still God. There is still hope. We still matter to Him. The Holy Spirit still lives in us. The Bible is still true. The church is still intact. Heaven still awaits. And in that we can rejoice.

What does this mean for the sexually abused woman described at the beginning of this session? It means she can pound her clenched fists on the table and scream, "God, why didn't You stop my father? Why did You let him hurt me again and again? If You're a loving God, how could You stand to watch it happen? Are You so powerless that You couldn't do anything about it? Or are You simply not there at all?"

For a woman as violently abused as that woman was, those are inevitable questions. Emotional authenticity demands that she ask them. And it demands that she ask them over and over again, for however long it takes her to reestablish genuine faith in God. If she doesn't, she'll become an inauthentic Christian who goes through the motions of believing in God but has no inner confidence in His power or love.

If you were to look in my journal, you would find my frustrations, fears, and questions spilled all over its pages. But you'd also find a written record of the assurances and promises God has given me in return. The day after my father's death, I poured out my fear to the Lord. I knew I was facing the greatest ministry challenges I had ever faced. How could I face them without the person who had been my greatest cheerleader, the one who had always made me believe I could handle anything? God answered my heart's cry by assuring me that if I would abide in Him, He would become my encourager. He would make me strong.

*Discuss it with someone else*—There is healing power—a release, a catharsis—in sharing our inner hurts with someone else that makes the burden seem lighter. Sometimes just having someone affirm the legitimacy of our pain eases it a little. There's also the obvious benefit of receiving guidance from those with whom we share. Overwhelming issues suddenly become manageable when a friend offers an insight or suggests a course of action we hadn't thought of.

*Seek professional help*—This step was needed for each of the people described in the first pages of this session. The victim of sexual abuse had experienced such extreme violation that it took years of intense therapy to heal the damage. The other woman had created such a convincing image of toughness and invincibility that only a trained counselor could trace her uncontrollable tears to years of buried grief. And only a person trained to deal with compulsive behaviors could uncover the unmet needs driving the successful businessman to overeat himself into obesity.

God doesn't ask us to spiritualize these and other painful realities away. The healing process requires divine intervention and spiritual growth. Loving family and friends can provide the human support and wisdom we need. But there are times when competent Christian counselors are needed to help us uncover and understand significant events in our past, resolve tensions, and initiate more positive relationships with significant people in our lives.

## PUTTING YOURSELF IN THE PICTURE

Challenge group members to take time in the coming week to use part or all of this application section as an opportunity for continued growth.

# Unstereotyping Evangelism

## Luke 15:3—7

### Introduction

The topic of authentic evangelism may be threatening for many people. Many of us have had bad experiences with people trying to evangelize us or pressuring us with guilt to do evangelism in a way completely contrary to how God has wired us. Let your group members know that this session is not about guilt-centered pressure or commando tactics for attacking their friends with the Gospel.

Let them know the focus will be on growing in our commitment to reach out to seekers in a way that best fits who we are and how God has made us. When we do evangelism in a manner consistent with how God has wired us, it can be the most exciting and rewarding part of our life of faith.

### The Big Picture

Take time to read this introduction with the group. There are suggestions for how this can be done in the beginning of this leader's section.

### A Biblical Portrait

**Read Luke 15:3–7**

### Sharpening the Focus

**Read Snapshot "What Motivates You?" before Question 3**

**Question Three** Second Kings 6–7 records the story of the king of Aram's siege of Samaria. Because of the siege and a great famine in the land, the city experienced a food shortage so severe it drove the people to cannibalism. To survive, mothers literally ate their children. Doomed to die with the rest of the city, four outcast lepers decided on a desperate plan: to enter the camp of the Arameans and surrender. They said, "If they spare us, we live; if they kill us, then we die" (2 Kings 7:4).

To their amazement, the lepers found the camp deserted. God had caused the Aramean army "to hear the sound of chariots and horses and a great army" (2 Kings 7:6). The Arameans concluded that the king of Israel had hired the Hittites and Egyptians to attack them. Terrified, they fled for their lives, leaving everything in the camp behind.

The lepers were beside themselves! They rushed from tent to tent, feasting and looting. They filled their arms with treasures of silver and gold and gathered mounds of clothes that would last them for years. Hurriedly they hid their plunder, then ran back for more.

But their frantic hoarding was cut short. "We're not doing right. This is a day of good news and we are keeping it to ourselves. . . . Let's go at once and report this to the royal palace" (2 Kings 7:9). They did, and the entire city enjoyed the abundance of the Aramean camp.

Why did the lepers share the secret of the abandoned camp? Because of the "stockpile factor." They were overwhelmed by their unexpected good fortune. They were awed by the provision divinely supplied for them. They knew it was a crime to keep the incredible bounty of God's blessing all to themselves.

When true believers are awed by the greatness of God and the privilege of becoming His children, they become sincerely motivated, effective evangelists. They find themselves saying naturally with the psalmist, "Taste and see that the Lord is good" (Ps. 34:8). With little strategy or effort, they find fitting opportunities to share with seekers their confidence in God's goodness, wisdom, and power. "I don't know about you," they say, "but I've found God to be so wonderful, I would be a fool not to serve Him."

Why aren't more believers motivated by the "stockpile factor"? Because Satan does everything in his power to convince spiritual princes that they're paupers. If he can make us lose sight of our wealth, he can render us ineffective as evangelists.

That is why each of us needs a daily refresher course on the scope of our blessings. One way that happens for me is by keeping a journal and writing out my thanks to God. Every time I go over my stockpile, I become filled with a sense of spiritual wonder. I think, "Why would anyone *not* want to be in a relationship with our wonderful God?" That makes for confident evangelism.

**Question Four** There are many things that can motivate us to tell others about God's love and faith in Jesus Christ.

One powerful motivation for personal evangelism is *the honor of being an agent of God*. Jesus told His followers, "But you will receive power when the Holy Spirit comes on you; and you will be my witnesses in Jerusalem, and in all Judea and Samaria, and to the ends of the earth" (Acts 1:8).

As remarkable as it seems, God chooses ordinary people to be His spokespersons. To every believer like you or me He says, "You are My special agent. You are the person I need to reach a certain group of humans in a corner of My world. They need your personality, your abilities, your perspective on life, your age factor, your sense of humor, and your message. They need *you*, filled with the Holy Spirit and commissioned as My agent of peace and reconciliation." That commission motivates me!

What's the key to being effectively used by God? A humble, submissive heart tuned in to the Holy Spirit. Jesus said, "You will receive power when the Holy Spirit has come upon you." When I'm preoccupied with my own agenda, I may stumble upon few opportunities to be God's spokesperson. But if I quiet myself in the morning, give my day to the Lord, and ask Him to work through me, I often find many opportunities and sense God's power at work.

Another motivation for becoming an effective evangelist is one I'd rather not mention: *the reality of hell*. I hate thinking about it, teaching about it, and writing about it. But the plain truth is that hell *is* real and real people go there for eternity.

The reality of hell was a major theme in Jesus' evangelistic ministry. Jesus grieved over the rich young ruler because He knew he was walking the road to hell. He wept over the people of Jerusalem because He saw them as sheep without a Shepherd; it was only a matter of time before they'd wander off the cliffs of eternity and into hell's abyss. He narrated incidents like Lazarus and the rich man (Luke 16:19–31), which plainly told of the agony and desperation of those forever separated from God.

Jesus confronted the Pharisees, the scribes, the tax-gatherers, the politicians, the rich, the poor—anybody and everybody—with the hard truth: Unless they repented and put their faith in Him, they would die in their sin and face eternal condemnation.

Why did Jesus teach from early morning until late at night? Why did He square off against the critics and endure the ridicule? Because it broke His heart to see people headed for hell.

I believe in hell. I believe in it rationally; I believe in it emotionally. I'm not neurotic about it, but I have to admit that it impacts me every day. It bothers me. It jars me out of complacency. It sparks my energies.

Sometimes people ask why the elders of our church place so much emphasis on reaching the nonchurched. Why do we pour so much time, energy, and money into programs, ideas, and additional staff directed toward outreach? Because when you truly believe in hell, you develop a "whatever it takes" mentality. You realize that the stakes are sky-high. You're not just playing church—eternal life and death hang in the balance.

The final motivation for evangelism I want to look at is *the reward of leading someone to Christ.* It is a wonderful feeling to have someone say to you, "You know, I was lost until God brought His message to me through you. Thanks for reaching out to me, answering my questions, and putting up with my rebellion. Thanks for loving me when I wasn't very lovable. Thanks for living a life that matched your message. Thanks for leading me to the God of grace!" Scripture tells us that heaven throws a party for every seeker who submits to Christ (Luke 15:3–7). What a thrill to be a part of the cosmic celebration.

**Read Snapshot "Major in the People Business" before Question 5**

**Question Six** One of my favorite passages that shows Jesus' emphasis on the ultimate importance of people is Luke 15. According to this passage, the religious leaders were upset because Jesus, who claimed to be the holy Son of God, was hanging around with sinners, sharing meals with cheating tax collectors, arrogant merchants, filthy-mouthed tentmakers, even prostitutes! When Jesus heard the scribes and Pharisees grumbling about His unacceptable associations, He decided to let them know once and for all just how much He loved the very sinners they despised.

He told three moving stories about a lost sheep, a lost coin, and a prodigal son. In each of the stories something of great value is lost, and the thing that is lost matters so much to its owner that he or she warrants either an all-out search or an anguished vigil. When at last the sheep and coin are found and the son returns home, the respective households burst into songs of rejoicing. Jesus says, "In the same way, I tell you, there is rejoicing in the presence of the angels of God over one sinner who repents" (Luke 15:10).

What is Jesus' message? That lost, wayward, rebellious, cursing people matter to God so much that He wants us to go after them. He wants us to search them out and bring them to Him.

Authentic evangelism flows from a mind-set that acknowledges the ultimate value of people—forgotten people, lost people, wandering people, up-and-out people, down-and-out people. God calls us to love them, serve them, and reach them. Everything else goes up in smoke.

### Read Snapshot "What's Your Style?" before Question 7

**Question Seven** This section briefly reviews six styles of evangelism. If your group desires to study the topic of personal evangelism in greater depth you may want to consider using the *Becoming a Contagious Christian* materials (a book, as well as a complete training curriculum with Leader's Guide, Participant's Guide, and video that includes "slice of life" dramas by the Willow Creek Drama Team). Also, there is a six-week small group study in this *Interactions* series called *Reaching Out: Sharing God's Love Naturally*.

*Confrontational Style*—Peter, the transformed fisherman, had a confrontational style of evangelism. "Listen carefully to what I say," Peter began in his dynamic Pentecost sermon in Acts 2. He then proceeded to explain Jesus' fulfillment of the ancient Scriptures and His identity as the Christ. In conclusion, he said, "Therefore let all Israel be assured of this: God has made this Jesus, whom you crucified, both Lord and Christ" (Acts 2:36). In other words, "You crucified the wrong man! You killed the Son of God!"

Pierced to the heart, the crowd asked Peter, "What shall we do?" Peter replied, "Repent and be baptized. . . . Save yourselves from this corrupt generation" (Acts 2:37–40).

Peter exhorted and challenged; he confidently charged in and hit the crowd with a frontal assault so effective that three thousand people trusted Christ that day (Acts 2:41). You see, some people will be reached only when they are confronted courageously and straightforwardly with their sin and their need to repent.

And Peter was just the person to do that. He was an "action" person. He was almost always the first person to speak, move, and act. We remember him as the one who walked on water and fell in, but he also was the only one who got out of the boat, the only one willing to take the first step. In the Garden, when Jesus was arrested, Peter grabbed a sword and whacked off a guy's ear. He loved to create action, to stir up controversy.

It didn't bother him at all to stand up in front of the masses on Pentecost Day and create a little havoc.

Some people will only come to Christ if they are "knocked over the head with truth" by someone like Peter. Fortunately, God has equipped certain believers with the combination of personality, gifts, and desires that make it natural for them to confront others.

If God has made you this way, then get out there and confront people with God's truth. Offer your personality and passion to the Lord, and ask the Holy Spirit to surround your natural confidence with sensitivity and discernment. Then pray that God will lead you to people who need someone to look them right in the eye and say, "Here's the truth. What are you going to do about it?"

*Intellectual Style*—Though he could be confrontational like Peter, the apostle Paul often used an intellectual approach to evangelism. In Acts 17 we read that Paul reasoned with the Jews and God-fearing Greeks, "explaining and proving" Christ's resurrection (Acts 17:3). He conversed with the intelligentsia and debated with the philosophers of Athens. In his famous sermon on Mars Hill, he ingeniously used the Athenians' altar to an unknown god as an introduction to his presentation of the true God.

I can imagine Peter in Athens. "What's wrong with you people? Tear down that altar to an unknown god! Repent and worship the true God!" His confrontational approach would never have worked with the intellectuals. They needed a more persuasive, academic approach, like Paul's. We read that in Thessalonica, "Some of the Jews were persuaded and joined Paul and Silas, as did a large number of God-fearing Greeks and not a few prominent women" (Acts 17:4). In Athens, likewise, "A few men became followers of Paul and believed. . . . also a woman named Damaris, and a number of others" (Acts 17:34).

Paul was highly educated, extremely intelligent, and capable of putting together cogent arguments. By nature he loved analyzing, studying, contemplating, and reasoning. He knew that some people needed to grapple with tough questions before they could come to faith in Christ.

What about you? Could you be an intellectual evangelist? Are you an effective debater? Do you enjoy examining evidence and reasoning through to a conclusion? Do you like to wrestle with difficult questions? Do you love it when cultists come to your door? Then take your calling as an intellectual evangelist seriously. Read, study, and train yourself.

*Testimonial Style*—John 9 records Jesus' healing of a blind beggar. Well-known to the community because of his impertinent begging, the healed man became the center of a controversy.

Neighbors questioned if he really was the same man they'd seen begging since his birth. Pharisees wondered who healed him and questioned the godliness of someone who would heal on the Sabbath. Others concluded that only a sinless man could perform such deeds. Finally, they asked the blind man himself what he thought of his healer. His answer was pure and simple, "One thing I do know. I was blind but now I see!" (John 9:25).

The man's simple testimonial only piqued more controversy, so he expanded his explanation. "Nobody has ever heard of opening the eyes of a man born blind. If this man were not from God, he could do nothing" (John 9:32–33). "Draw your own conclusions," he seemed to say, "I've drawn mine."

Testimonial style evangelists neither confront nor intellectualize; they simply tell the story of the miraculous work of Jesus Christ in their lives. They say, "I was spiritually blind, but now I see. Jesus Christ changed my life, and He can change yours."

What happens when seekers hear simple testimonies like that from people they respect? Sometimes nothing happens. Sometimes they say, "That's great for you, Dave. Now can we order our meal?" But sometimes they begin to think. Sometimes they say, "Wait a minute, I thought I was a Christian too— for all those same reasons. I better learn more about this."

In the *Becoming a Contagious Christian* evangelism seminars at our church we strongly encourage people to write out a brief testimony and become familiar enough with it that they can present it clearly and comfortably. We've found that being prepared with a concise, non-preachy explanation of their conversion frees them to witness effectively in the settings the Holy Spirit orchestrates. Many seekers don't need to hear a sermon; they just need a solid, normal Christian to share with them a slice of their transformed life.

*Interpersonal Style*—When Matthew came to faith, he came up with the idea of throwing a party strategically designed to get his unsaved tax collector friends to rub shoulders with Jesus and the disciples. I like to call this a "party with a purpose" or a "Matthew Party." Although we all need to build relationships with those we hope to reach, those with the interpersonal approach specialize in this area by building deeper relationships with many people.

Is God calling you to be an evangelist right where you are? Do you have friends and family members who don't know the Lord? If so, begin to pour your time, concern, and prayers in their direction. Make yourself available to be God's personal agent to them.

*Invitational Style*—Most people are familiar with the story of the Samaritan woman at the well (John 4). After a lengthy conversation with Jesus, she became convinced that He was the Son of God. Excited, she left her water pots and ran into the city. Instead of trying to recreate the conversation in her own words, she begged the people of the city to come to the well and hear Jesus for themselves. They did, and verse 39 tells us that many of the Samaritans believed in Him.

The Samaritan woman was an invitational evangelist. She knew she wasn't prepared to articulate the message in a powerful way, so she invited her friends and acquaintances to come and hear someone who could explain it more effectively.

Many people condemn themselves because they're not confrontational or intellectual, they don't have a dramatic testimony to share, and they're not particularly relational. They feel they have nothing to offer as an evangelist. Perhaps God wants them to do just what the woman at the well did: Invite people to "come and hear."

Fifty percent of the people who write to tell me about their conversion experience say something like this: "I was lost. I was confused. I was lonely. Then someone invited me to a Sunday service [or to a concert, a holiday service, a special event]. I kept coming back, and over time I came to the point of trusting Christ in a personal way."

Do you think you might be an invitational evangelist? Then get aggressive! Find out about Christian concerts and special events designed specifically for unbelievers. Couple your efforts with those of a church that provides opportunities for seekers and new believers. Use the valuable evangelistic style God has given you to make a mark for eternity.

*Serving Style*—One of the most endearing people in Scripture is a woman named Dorcas. She tremendously impacted her city by doing deeds of kindness, making garments for the poor and forgotten and distributing them in the name of Christ. She may never have knocked on a door; it's unlikely she ever preached a sermon. Yet through her acts of service she pointed people to the God who could transform human hearts and fill them with love (Acts 9).

Dorcas was a service evangelist. She used her unique serving gifts as tangible expressions of the Gospel message. Like her, you may have a tender spirit and helpful heart. You may have gifts of mercy, helps, hospitality, giving, and counseling. You may be a very effective evangelist as you connect sharing Christ with serving people.

Have you been intimidated by outspoken evangelists who make you feel like a second-class citizen because all you can do is "serve people"? Please don't feel that way. Serve with a joyful, compassionate heart and tell those you are serving, "I offer this service because I want you to know you matter to God." You will plant seeds that others can water and the Holy Spirit can bring to fruition. There are many unbelievers who are potentially open to becoming Christians. The one thing they lack is someone like you to soften their heart through your acts of service. Be that person for them!

## PUTTING YOURSELF IN THE PICTURE

Challenge group members to take time in the coming week to use part or all of this application section as an opportunity for continued growth.

# WORK: TURNING DRUDGERY INTO FULFILLMENT

## COLOSSIANS 3:23—24

### INTRODUCTION

Over the years I've met hundreds of people who can't wait to get up in the morning. I've met people who love being accountants, skilled craftsmen, commodities traders, schoolteachers, bank tellers, housecleaners, landscapers, hairstylists, mechanics, and every other kind of worker imaginable. The vitality and enthusiasm these people generate because of their love for their work positively affects their lives, spilling over into their marriages, parenting, friendships, and recreational pursuits.

I've also met hundreds of people whose dissatisfaction with their jobs casts a shadow over every other dimension of life. They may earn the same money, enjoy the same prestige, and have the same job description as their satisfied counterparts, but they're unhappy and frustrated. They take out their unhappiness on the kids and the dog, and they walk through life in a haze of bitterness and lethargy. They can't wait to throw off the weight of their labors.

What determines the difference? How can two people share the same job, and one be joy-filled and energetic, while the other is unhappy and drained? The key is vocational authenticity, which means we have the right job, for the right reason, and enjoy the right rewards.

It will be important to clarify at the beginning of this session that work is much broader than a nine-to-five office job. For some people in your group, the primary workplace is in the home caring for a family; for others, it might be their commitment to a college education. Be sure all those in your group know that their form of work is important, and that God wants them to do their work for His glory.

## THE BIG PICTURE

Take time to read this introduction with the group. There are suggestions for how this can be done in the beginning of this section.

## A WIDE ANGLE VIEW

**Question One** Some people hate their work and see it as a form of curse they have to endure. But human labor is no more God's curse than life itself. Though the Fall did lead to consequences that tainted work, we musn't forget that God introduced the concept of human labor *before* the Fall. When Adam and Eve were still innocent of sin, God gave them a job to do. He called Adam to name the animals, then asked Adam and Eve to subdue the animals, manage the Garden of Eden, and prepare food from the plants and trees He had provided.

Why would a loving God put His children to work as soon as He created them? Because He knew human labor was a blessing. He knew it would provide them challenges, excitement, adventure, and rewards that nothing else would. He knew that creatures made in His image needed to devote their time to meaningful tasks.

The writer of Ecclesiastes understood this when he wrote, "Then I realized that it is good and proper for a man to eat and drink, and to find satisfaction in his toilsome labor under the sun during the few days of life God has given him—for this is his lot" (Eccl. 5:18). This writer understood that if we have enough to eat and drink, and if we enjoy our work, we are blessed people.

## A BIBLICAL PORTRAIT

### Read Colossians 3:23–24

**Question Two** An essential requirement for an authentic job life is that we do our work for the right reason: to please and glorify God. When a Christian walks on the job site, she should be thinking about more than making money, impressing her boss, or even how much she enjoys her work. She should be conjuring up ways to honor God through her marketplace endeavors.

Wherever we work, whatever our job description, our ultimate boss is Jesus Christ. He's the one we need to please. When we do, our work becomes a source of worship. Our job site becomes a temple. Each project we undertake becomes an offering to God.

Sharpening the Focus

### Read Snapshot "What Turns Your Crank?" before Question 3

**Question Four** Be conscious of your time limits when asking people in your group to relate their ideal job description. You may want to ask just three or four people to do this.

When I was in youth ministry, one high school student emerged as an unusually gifted leader. When we divided the youth group into subgroups called teams, his team always developed the strongest identity and attracted the greatest number of new kids. He seemed to have a special knack for organizing, inspiring, and leading others. He eventually joined the management team at our church, overseeing nearly one hundred members of our pastoral staff. He's an extremely effective manager because his responsibilities are consistent with his God-given abilities.

Our director of programming also grew up in our youth group and exhibited her natural aptitudes at an early age. In grade school she staged plays and musicals in her basement, taking shades off lamps to make spotlights, rearranging furniture to design sets, and raiding closets to create one-of-a-kind costumes. Then she invited neighbor kids to come and watch. In high school, instead of being *in* the school variety shows, she *produced* them. In college, she studied communication arts. Now she coordinates the music, drama, media, and production departments at our church and is responsible for programming our midweek and weekend services.

I also know a salesman who could sell ice to an Eskimo, sand to a Bedouin, or anything to a Dutchman. (Being Dutch, I know what a challenge that is.) He describes himself as a kid who enjoyed highly social kinds of play, loved competition, and was always the life of the party. He was easily bored and needed constant challenge and stimulation. He was never happier than when he sold his sister's Girl Scout cookies door-to-door! Is it any wonder he's a successful salesman today?

But let's take that same relational, competitive, high-energy guy, roll the years ahead, and make him the assistant librarian in the township library. How would you predict his job satisfaction level? I think he would last about two weeks—even if the job offered great pay and unbelievable perks. It wouldn't meet his need for action, competition, and variety; it wouldn't be in sync with his motivated abilities.

God intends our work to be a natural expression of who we are, consistent with our inherent interests and abilities. When it isn't, we feel out of place, insignificant, and either bored or defeated. When it is, we feel as if we have something important to contribute, and we're challenged without being overwhelmed.

My daughter loves to sing and dance and act. When she was a young girl she performed in a musical production. As I tucked her into bed that night, she said, "You know, Dad, I feel like I really come to life when I'm singing and dancing. That's when I *live*." God wants each of us to have that kind of response to our life's work. He wants our labors to energize us and pump vitality into our daily lives.

Are your labors consistent with your God-given uniqueness and your motivated abilities? If you can't answer yes, or if you've never identified your motivated abilities, please visit a career counselor, take a vocational aptitude test, or read one of the excellent books on this subject. Two books I suggest are *Finding a Job You Can Love* by Ralph Mattson and Arthur Miller (Thomas Nelson) and *What Color Is Your Parachute?* by Richard Nelson Bolles (Ten Speed Press).

Before deciding on a career, everyone ought to answer the "What turns your crank?" question. When we interview prospective church employees, we put it this way: "If you could wave a wand and write your own job description, what would you write? What do you love to do more than anything else? What do you feel you're best at? How do you like to spend your vocational time?" We know that if we can shape a position closely consistent with those natural desires, we'll have an enthusiastic, satisfied, effective worker.

Extenuating circumstances sometimes force us to settle for jobs outside our range of interests and strengths, but to the extent we can, we should view those jobs as temporary. God wants each of us to enjoy vocational authenticity, which begins with having a job consistent with our God-given motivated abilities.

### Read Snapshot "How We Work Matters More Than We Know" before Question 5

### Read Snapshot "Setting a New Standard" before Question 6

**Question Six** Once we've established ourselves as valuable assets and credible workers, we're free to honor God on a more personal level: by who we are and how we behave in marketplace relationships.

It goes without saying that Christians must *exhibit personal integrity* in the marketplace. We must shun, without exception, unethical business practices and financial improprieties, even violations as commonplace as making unauthorized calls on business phones or being careless with expense accounts. Christians must strive every day to be beyond reproach in all their marketplace dealings and practices.

It is alarmingly easy for sincere believers to slip into self-centeredness. I know. Time and again I've gotten so consumed with message preparation or administrative responsibilities that I've passed a staff member in the hallway, glimpsed a look of pain or frustration, and walked on, telling myself I am too busy to respond. "Hope he works it out," I'd think. "Hope someone can help her." Often I've been chastised by the inner voice of the Holy Spirit: "Who do you think you are? Where is the likeness of Christ I ought to see in you? Have you forgotten what's really important?"

Marketplace mentality is notoriously self-centered and survivalistic. Christians have the opportunity to change the marketplace by overturning that modus operandi, by *acting like brothers and sisters* to their coworkers rather than cutthroat competitors.

Philippians 2:4 says, "Each of you should look not only to your own interests, but also to the interests of others." In the marketplace that means we need to *make* time to express interest in others—in their spouse, kids, health, problems, goals, frustrations, hobbies, vacations, and dreams. Competitors don't care about those things, but brothers and sisters do.

We also need *to be helpers* in the marketplace. That may mean offering to take up slack in another worker's load. It may mean staying late to help a partner finish a report or occasionally working through lunch to help someone meet a deadline.

Honoring God also requires Christians *to be vulnerable* in the marketplace. That means admitting to wrongdoing and saying, "Look, I was feeling pressed and I took it out on you. I said things I shouldn't have. I'm sorry. Please forgive me." Let's face it. Even the most devout Christian is going to blow it now and then. We're going to make mistakes, use poor judgment, lose our temper, speak unkindly about someone, and fail to meet work standards. The important question is, What do we do then? Do we try to rationalize misbehavior? Do we throw the blame on someone else? Do we cover it up?

Contrary to what many Christians think, we do not have to be perfect to have integrity with unbelievers. We don't have to be plastic caricatures with painted smiles. We need to be human—sincere, honest, transparent, humble—real people who make mistakes, admit them, and then move on.

Finally, we honor God *by being reconcilers*. More doors have been slammed, names called, and conversations coldly terminated in the marketplace than anywhere else. Rampant relational breakdown is almost a given. Christians honor God by entering that relational war zone as agents of reconciliation. That doesn't mean they avoid conflict; it means they apply the principles of relational authenticity. They enter the tunnel of chaos, and even lead others there when necessary, knowing that openly dealing with hostility and misunderstanding is the only path to harmony.

Honoring God by who you are in the marketplace is no easy task. It demands a radical flip-flop of values and a die-hard determination to row upstream. But it offers the potential to bring the impact of integrity and the touch of compassion to an environment often devoid of both.

### Read Snapshot "What We Say Has Eternal Consequences" before Question 7

**Question Seven** Christians have often been ineffective in our attempts to make an eternal impact because we have neglected the first two steps in honoring God in the marketplace: either we have been careless workers whose shoddy methods and inferior standards offended coworkers, or we have been inconsistent Christians whose behavior was shaped more by marketplace mind-set than the mind of Christ. In either case, we've forfeited our credibility and turned an opportunity into a closed door.

What a shame! For eight hours a day, five days a week, Christians rub shoulders with men and women who matter to God and desperately need to hear more about Him. Paul aptly wrote, "How can they believe in the one of whom they have not heard? And how can they hear without someone preaching to them?" (Rom. 10:14). At work we can be that "someone" who can tell them the message of the Gospel.

Jesus never commanded us to engage in theological debates with strangers, flaunt four-inch crosses and Jesus stickers, or throw out Christian catch phrases. But He did tell us to work and live in such a way that when the Holy Spirit orchestrates opportunities to speak about God, we will have earned the right to do so.

**Question Eight** Vocational authenticity means we pursue the right job (in line with our motivated abilities), for the right reason (to honor God), so that we enjoy the right rewards.

*Confidence*—Have you ever been served in a restaurant by a brand-new waiter or waitress? You can usually tell they are new by their obvious nervousness and awkwardness. They often spill water and deliver food in a clumsy, disorganized fashion. And they tend to be either preoccupied and unavailable or overly solicitous and bothersome.

But if you happen to come back to the same restaurant two weeks later, you'll likely see an amazing transformation. Gone is the self-conscious nervousness. They now adroitly balance four plates of food and a platter of drinks while weaving their way between crowded tables and bantering freely with pleased patrons. Their motions are fluid, their manner comfortable, and they radiate a sense of healthy confidence.

Confidence is one of the rewards of vocational authenticity. It develops in our lives when we accept marketplace challenges and stretch our abilities. Confidence in one's competence is a blessing of incalculable worth.

One of the most confident leaders in biblical history was King David, a self-assured leader, soldier, and statesman. Scripture gives some clues about how he developed that confidence. When David was just a small child, he was a shepherd. That meant he had to roam the countryside night and day, alone, to seek pastures and water for his sheep. All the while, he had to scan the hillsides to make sure no wild animals were lurking about. Scripture says that once a bear threatened the sheep, and David attacked and killed it. Later, he did the same thing to a lion.

When the need arose for a warrior to face the famed Goliath, David volunteered, citing his past success in defeating the bear and lion. When he became king, he overcame enemy armies and led Israel into its golden era.

Where did David get the confidence to be such a strong and able leader? I think the seeds were sown on the hillsides of Palestine, when he took his first job as a shepherd boy.

Few arenas make as rigorous demands on us as does the marketplace. It says, "Here's a challenge. It's up to you. Start in. Learn. Grow. Work hard. Get the job done." When we start, we feel uncomfortable and fearful. But as we become increasingly proficient in our tasks, those unpleasant sensations are gradually replaced by a satisfying sense of confidence. Almost without realizing it, we begin thinking, *God has given me gifts and abilities and talents. I have strengths and valuable skills. I'm a competent person. I have something to offer this company. I can do excellent work. I'm an important member of the team.*

Those moments of positive self-awareness are exactly what God had in mind for us to experience in the marketplace. He gave us abilities to invest in meaningful labor in part so we could receive the rich reward of self-confidence.

Lottery winners often find that lying on the beach is not all it's cracked up to be. God instituted human labor because He knew our confidence and self-esteem would soar not in the ease of long-term leisure, but in the pursuit of meaningful labor.

*Character development*—The second reward of diligent labor is improved character. I can easily trace the development of my greatest character strengths back to the years when I worked in my family's wholesale produce business.

My dad loved to work. And he loved to put his kids to work. When I was in grade school, he'd wake me up at 5:00 A.M. and take me to the warehouse to unload semis filled with produce that needed to be distributed to local hospitals, restaurants, and grocery stores.

On more than one occasion, after an hour or two hauling cases of oranges, tomatoes, or lettuce, I would jump down from the trailer to take a break, only to have Dad see me and ask, "Is that truck all unloaded? If it isn't, get back there and finish the job."

Later, he put me to work on company farms, planting and harvesting seed. During the crucial planting weeks we would work from early morning to late at night. Sometimes, in the middle of a burning afternoon, I'd cruise by the barn to refuel the tractor and ask if I could take a couple hours off to go water-skiing with my friends. He'd say, "Are you finished with the field? If not, get back to work. Finish the job, Son!"

At the time I thought many of his requests were unreasonable. I hated it when he said, "Finish the job." I thought his work ethic was way overdone! Now, more than ten years after his death, I thank God almost every day for using my dad and the marketplace to burn certain character qualities in my life. I may lack a lot in terms of natural ability and raw potential, but one thing I have in spades is the character quality of perseverance. I know how to finish the job.

What's great is that, like confidence, character improvements spill over into other areas of life. If I get frustrated when working through a relational difficulty, part of me says, "Give up.

Take a break. It's not worth it." But another part says, "Keep trying. Pursue reconciliation. Finish the job."

If I'm struggling with my relationship with God, unaware of His presence and uninspired in my attempts to journal and pray, part of me says, "Forget it. Try again tomorrow. It's not worth the effort." But another part of me says, "Keep pursuing. Keep listening. Finish the job."

The marketplace affords us the opportunity to develop every character quality God wants us to have. Are you enrolled in the marketplace classroom of character development? Do you look for opportunities on the job to practice godly virtues? When you get bogged down in a frustrating assignment, do you give up or see it as a chance to grow in perseverance? When tempted by an unethical practice, do you yield or see it as a chance to grow in honesty? When you hear a friend being slandered, do you give silent assent or stand up for your friend and practice loyalty?

The marketplace can provide graduate-level instruction in character development that can transform our lives and free us to be the men and women God wants us to be. It's up to us to use the opportunity and learn the lessons. Many people throw such opportunities away, but those who take advantage of them enjoy the unexpected reward of personal growth and maturity.

*Feeling of accomplishment*—When God completed His creative endeavors, He paused, looked over His handiwork, and said, "Behold! This is very good." Oozing from that divine statement is the blessed feeling of accomplishment. It's as though God were saying, "I conceived of this idea. I started the job. I stuck with it. I finished it. And I did it well." There's fulfillment in the completion of diligent labor.

Meaningful labor gives each of us the opportunity to enjoy the blessing of accomplishment. It provides a sweet reward to the salesman who closes the deal and silently screams, "I did it!"; to the janitor who puts away the cleaning equipment and surveys an immaculate facility; to the teacher who finishes the last lecture; to the farmer who harvests the last row; to the soprano who sings the last note of the concert; to the accountant who balances the last ledger; to the athlete who showers and leaves the stadium; to the architect who finishes the final drawings; to the mother who finally puts the baby down for the night; to the student who completes the final exam.

All of those moments are precious slices of reality reserved for people who labor diligently. When we engage in work that taps our God-given abilities, and when we do it to the best of our ability for God's honor, then we enjoy those blessed moments of accomplishment. Nothing beats that! I'm all for leisure-time activities, vacations, diversions, and breaks. They bring much-needed balance and sanity to our lives. But their greatest value is that they refresh us so we can resume our labors with greater energy, effectiveness, and creativity—and know greater accomplishment.

Human labor was designed by God, assigned to every one of us, and offered as an opportunity to build confidence, develop character, and enjoy the satisfaction of accomplishment. Does that sound like a curse?

Vocational authenticity, where we have the right job, for the right reason, and enjoy the right rewards, allows us to experience labor as the blessing it was meant to be.

## Putting Yourself in the Picture

Challenge group members to take time in the coming week to use part or all of this application section as an opportunity for continued growth.

## Note

Unfortunately, the blessing of work becomes a curse to those who allow their professions to become obsessions. Some people develop a psychological addiction to their work that causes them to alienate family and friends, neglect their health, and sabotage their spiritual lives. Though they seldom, if ever, admit that work is their god, it's obvious to others. Their job is what they live for, what they dream of, what they sacrifice all else for. For them the blessing of human labor becomes what the next drink is to the alcoholic. If you feel you might have one or more people in your group with this problem, invite them to meet with you and study the section in my book *Honest to God?* that discusses work life and spiritual life. It might also be helpful, with their permission, to invite a pastor or Christian counselor in on this process of evaluation.

# THE SEDUCTION OF MONEY

## 1 TIMOTHY 6:6—10

### INTRODUCTION

One of the greatest strategies of the Money Monster is to stay hidden. As long as we don't believe in its existence, we will continue to fall prey to its power.

When a child has irrational fears about monsters under the bed or hidden in the closet, we simply turn on the lights, do a quick inspection of the room and prove they don't exist. When people deny the existence of the Money Monster, we need to use a similar strategy. We need to turn a floodlight on our hearts and lives and expose the existence of this sinister monster.

This lesson will bring illumination to the dark corners of the hearts and closets of our lives. We will inspect those places where the Money Monster lives and we will serve him an eviction notice. In this session, we will ask tough questions to help group members honestly inspect their own lives and see where money has become a destructive force.

As you prepare to lead this session, pray for each group member and for yourself. Ask God to use His Word to help expose any area where money has become an unhealthy power in your life. Also, pray for each group member to be open and honest about the role money plays in their life. Pray for this to be a time when group members commit to do battle with the Money Monster and throw him out for good.

### THE BIG PICTURE

Take time to read this introduction with the group. There are suggestions for how this can be done in the beginning of the leader's section.

### A WIDE ANGLE VIEW

**Question One** There is a certain level of disclosure that comes with answering these questions. We live in a very materialistic age, and admitting this is a problem might be hard for some people. Allow group members an opportunity to begin identifying where they see the seduction of the Money Monster in their own lives and in their cultural setting.

## A Biblical Portrait

### Read 1 Timothy 6:6–10

**Question Three** The courts of spiritual bankruptcy are filled with men and women who vowed to get serious about their spiritual lives after one more deal, one more increase, one more level. Vast numbers have gained the whole world only to lose their souls because they believed the Money Monster's lies. Even sincere Christians have been lured by riches and the love of money and have squandered their lives and given up their spiritual fruitfulness.

The Money Monster's goal is to totally dominate our value system without our being aware of it. Unfortunately, we make it fairly easy for him to do that.

## Sharpening the Focus

### Read Snapshot "Michael's Story" before Question 4

**Question Four** We all know the story of the rich young ruler (Luke 18:18–30). Jesus' point in that story was that the young man would not be free to follow Him as long as he remained chained to the Money Monster. But the man was so dominated by the sinister power that he politely refused eternal life.

We shake our heads in disbelief, yet how many times have we similarly rejected a leading from God? A wonderful service opportunity comes our way, but before we say yes our mental calculators start crunching numbers. When the dollar total registers, the leash pulls tightly around our neck, and we say, "Ah, thanks God, but not this time. It'll cost me money. It'll decrease my net worth. I'd have to part with something. I can't, Lord. Not now. Maybe next time."

**Question Five** The Money Monster is alive and well and pulling out all the stops to get us under his control. He craftily offers his most lethal ploy as the harmless solution to all our financial woes. What is this deadly trap? Easy credit. For many people, hardly a day goes by that they don't get an offer in the mail for another credit card that will bring them financial freedom. What these credit companies ought to put on the cover of their letter is, "One simple step to financial bondage."

Never before has a culture been so committed to the "buy now, pay later" philosophy. Bumper stickers used to read, "It may not be much, but at least it's paid for." Now flashy imports sport this message, "I owe, I owe, so off to work I go!" I recently saw a bumper sticker in San Diego that said, "I want it all, and I want it now." For too many people, the key to having it all now is easy credit.

My introduction to this mentality came when I was about seven. I was riding with my dad in his pick-up truck, and we passed a farmhouse with a beautiful new luxury car in the driveway. It was white with a vinyl top and had wire wheel covers. It literally glistened in the sun. I said, "Look, Dad. That farmer must be really *rich*." He smiled and said, "Billy, that man is nearly busted. He owes money to everyone in this county, including me." I remember thinking, "That man is goofed up! Why would he buy a car he can't afford?"

As if reading my mind, Dad began an informal lecture frequently given in Dutch homes. "Here's the problem with people today, Billy. They tend to spend more money than they earn. Let's say a young fellow gets a job and makes a down payment on a new Volkswagen. He can barely afford the monthly payments, but he's convinced he needs that car.

"Two years later he gets a raise, but instead of paying off his Volkswagen, he trades it in on a Ford convertible. Now he's deeper in debt and his monthly payments are even higher, but at least he's having fun in his convertible. After two more years, he gets another raise. This time he trades his convertible in for a luxury model. Now he owes a ton of money and the monthly payments have gone through the roof! But all that matters to him is that he's driving a Lincoln. That's the problem with people today, Billy."

Unfortunately, few people today listen to homespun wisdom like that. Deceptive advertising feeds the belief that we can charge to the hilt and not get caught. An ad for a recent car promotion said, "No money down and no payments for three months." The buyer is almost lulled into believing the car is free—until he gets a payment book as thick as his Bible.

It used to be necessary to qualify for credit cards. Now the average person receives a steady stream of these plastic money-eaters in the mail. What happens? Buyers become enslaved to them. A woman once came to me in abject despair because she'd just learned she couldn't use her Visa to pay off Master Card.

Proverbs 22:7 says, "The borrower is servant to the lender." It's true. Pay-later schemes and credit cards have led hundreds of thousands of sincere Christians into financial bondage. And it destroys them! Some of the most anxious people I know are people who have slid down the icy slope of overspending into the deep, cold valley of debt. Now they're shivering at the bottom of the valley, realizing it may take months or years to regain a position of solvency. They never intended to end up in that valley; they're not bad people. They just got sucked into the lure of easy credit.

## Read Snapshot "What's Your Central Reality?" before Question 6

**Question Six** The question we need to ask is, "Which god is worth our ultimate allegiance?" Many people say, "If only I had a bigger house, a newer car, a longer vacation . . . then I'd be satisfied." I recently met a millionaire who'd achieved all his financial goals by the age of forty-two. Then he experienced "success panic." He sat in his condo in Palm Springs and suddenly realized his long list of acquisitions didn't satisfy.

If our central value is the acquisition of material goods, we'll have a hard time living within our means, because we'll never satiate our hunger for more. Material gain never delivers what it promises. Whether we know it or not, what we're really after is *soul* satisfaction. And no home, car, toy, or bank account can provide that.

## Read Snapshot "A Cheerful Giver" before Question 7

**Question Seven** The answer to this question is found in the Bible's perspective on giving. We read, "'Bring the whole tithe into the storehouse, that there may be food in my house. Test me in this,' says the LORD Almighty, 'and see if I will not throw open the floodgates of heaven and pour out so much blessing that you will not have room enough for it. I will prevent pests from devouring your crops, and the vines in your fields will not cast their fruit'" (Mal. 3:10–11). According to Scripture, the call to tithe is accompanied by the promise that God will intervene supernaturally in the financial affairs (crops and vines) of those who consistently do. They will enjoy financial miracles that would not happen if they neglected to give to God. Therefore, giving money to God should be viewed not as a debt we owe, but as a seed we sow.

In one of the key biblical passages regarding our need to give to God, Paul relates principles of giving to principles of farming. He says, "Remember this: Whoever sows sparingly will also reap sparingly, and whoever sows generously will also reap generously" (2 Cor. 9:6). What is Paul telling us about tithing through the agricultural habits of an unidentified farmer? He is telling us about the principles of investment, increase, and interval.

Every farmer is aware of the principle of *investment*: If he wants to harvest a crop, he needs to buy seed and plant it. No seed, no harvest. In the same way, we need to view tithing as an investment in the work of God *and* in our own personal financial freedom, since God blesses our giving spiritually and materially.

The farmer also understands the principle of *increase*: He will reap far more than he sows. A farmer who sows two bushels of wheat can expect to reap sixty-seven bushels. Three bushels of oats will yield seventy-nine bushels. In Malachi 3:10 God promises "so much blessing that you will not have room enough for it." Jesus said, "Give, and it will be given to you. A good measure, pressed down, shaken together and running over, will be poured into your lap" (Luke 6:38).

God always promises an abundant reward to those who sow the seeds of giving. Does that mean everyone who tithes will get rich? Some people think so. They preach a prosperity theology, which in its exaggerated form piggybacks the hedonistic American mind-set and seeks to obligate God to prosper them financially.

Prosperity theology is a questionable theology for two reasons. First, the spirit of biblical teaching on giving is that we give as a multifaceted expression of worship and obedience. Scripture never promotes a "give to get rich" mentality. Second, prosperity theology limits God's provision to monetary increase. In reality, God has many creative ways to honor the seeds we sow.

A young man told me of the frustration of driving an old, dilapidated car that was inadequate for the daily two-hour hospital trips necessitated by his infant daughter's chronic illness. "We couldn't afford a new car," he said, "and we didn't tell anyone we needed one. We just continued giving the tithe we'd always given, and trusted God to meet our need." Within weeks, a group of friends from church presented him with the keys to a dependable, late-model van. Through a miraculous set of circumstances, they had discovered his need and were able to raise the money to meet it.

Finally, the farmer knows about the principle of *interval*: He doesn't plant seed one day and harvest it the next. He patiently waits for it to mature in its own time.

Increase comes only after a reasonable interval. Too many people try to test God by saying, "Okay, I'll tithe this week. But if I don't see the increase by next week, that's it. Never again!" That approach proves two things. It proves that a person is trapped in a "give to get" mentality and has no interest in giving as an expression of worship and obedience. It also proves he has a lot to learn about trust. Trust means we patiently wait without doubting the outcome. We obey even when we don't see immediate rewards. The principle of interval gives us the chance to prove our trust.

I believe most true Christians would like to tithe. Deep inside they know they should. What stops them? The numbers. They trip over the math. It doesn't make sense to believe that the first step to financial freedom is to give money away. If you told that to your accountant, he'd think you were crazy!

But in God's economy, it works. He says, "You trust Me with your eternal destiny. You trust Me for daily guidance and wisdom. Now trust Me with your money. I won't let you down. Sow seeds of faith and I'll meet your needs abundantly."

There are several positive results of tithing. First, churches can finance their ministries without having to resort to manipulative arm-twisting, cheap gimmicks, or secular fund-raising schemes. Second, those who tithe enjoy the benefits of divine intervention in their financial affairs. And third, the Money Monster suffers a direct hit! Giving money away is like spitting in his face. Nothing makes him shriek with agony more than the smiles on our faces as we write out our checks for God's work. In writing them, we break the grip of his leash and enjoy the taste of freedom.

Several years ago I went to India to speak at an evangelistic crusade. The peasants there were so poor they had to spend all their rupees on food, and I commented to a church leader that they must be frustrated by their inability to give. He said, "Oh no, they *do* give. Twice a day they boil rice for the family meal. Each time they scoop out what they need, then put one scoop in a bag. By the end of the week they have fourteen scoops of rice, which they put in the offering to be distributed to the needy."

With nothing to draw from but their own lack, these peasants choked the hoarding spirit of greed by giving what they could. If we want to defeat it, we must do the same.

You might find it helpful to have some responses to some of the common questions that might come up in this discussion:

1. Should I tithe on my gross or net earnings?

I believe that's open to choice, but remember: "If you sow bountifully, you'll reap bountifully; if you sow sparingly, you'll reap sparingly."

2. Where should I direct the ten percent?

Scripture teaches a concept called "storehouse tithing" (Mal. 3), which implies we should give our tithe to the local fellowship God has called us to join. Giving beyond the ten percent is "free will" giving and can be directed anywhere.

3. Should I tithe if I am deeply in debt and unable to pay creditors on time?

Our elders usually counsel people whose finances are in disarray to give a lower percentage until they reduce their debt enough that they're not compromising their witness to creditors.

4. Should I tithe if my spouse is adamantly opposed to it?

Giving should be a cheerful, worshipful experience. It should never become a wedge in a marriage relationship. Communicate to your spouse how strongly you feel about tithing and try to work out a compromise so you can give some portion of your income without alienating your spouse.

### Read Snapshot "Save, Save, Save—How to Pay Yourself" before Question 8

**Question Eight** Most people would rather buy lottery tickets than put away ten percent each week. Let's face it, it takes discipline to keep from spending money. It takes willpower to say no to tempting purchases. It takes commitment to the principle of delayed gratification—enduring hardship now for the payoff later.

Too many young couples yield to the temptation to spend their limited excess. Then, when they incur unexpected expenses, they have to borrow. This often begins their downward spiral into long-term indebtedness.

Proverbs 6:6–8 says, "Go to the ant, you sluggard [lazy man]; consider its ways and be wise! It has no commander, no overseer or ruler, yet it stores its provisions in summer and gathers its food at harvest."

In other words, mimic the ant: Set aside a freedom stash in summer, so you'll be prepared for the winter. Another proverb says, "In the house of the wise are stores of choice food and oil, but a foolish man devours all he has" (Prov. 21:20). This is a creative way of saying the wise man saves, while the foolish man spends everything he has.

Money management forces us into the graduate school of character. It's hard to say no to immediate gratification. But if we cut class, if we drop out, if we're shortsighted, we'll play right into the Money Monster's trap and end up in financial frustration.

Giving God ten percent and saving ten percent leaves eighty percent to live on—eighty percent to pay the bills. It's at precisely this point most people cave in. Usually it's not that they *can't* live on eighty percent; it's simply that they *won't*. They refuse to limit their living expenses. They allow glittering temptations and social pressures to push them into a standard of living that eats up all their money.

Rather then altering their lifestyle—living in a smaller house, driving an older car, buying fewer clothes, joining a food co-op—they eliminate tithing and saving. In so doing, they close the door to God's supernatural involvement in their finances and eliminate the freedom fund that would help cover future expenses.

It's bad enough that they're spending *everything* they earn. What's worse is that it's only a matter of time before they'll be spending *more* than they earn. The first emergency or unexpected expense will put them over the edge into indebtedness.

Few people would consider driving without a gas gauge, because they know the dangers and inconveniences associated with running out of gas. Yet most people operate their personal finances without a spending gauge. They casually spend from day to day, and when they run out of money by the middle of the month, they say, "Oops! We're out. Now what do we do?"

The only way to avoid that is to use a budget. Though it's one of the most unpopular concepts in contemporary America, it's the only way to live within fixed boundaries. Every January Lynne and I agree on a realistic, workable budget. First we deduct our giving and saving. Then we deduct our set monthly expenses (utilities, mortgage, insurance, taxes, food). Finally, we determine how much we can spend on negotiable expenses (clothing, gifts, vacations, household improvements, entertainment). Then we record these set amounts and agree together not to spend beyond them.

We don't enjoy sticking with a budget any more than anyone else does. But we do enjoy the financial freedom that accompanies it, the security of knowing we're not going to run out of money before the end of the month or be caught off guard by unexpected expenses.

There is not one economic lifestyle that's right for every believer. Teachers who make sweeping generalizations about how all Christians should spend their money are adding to Scripture. The Bible paints the ideal financial picture in broad strokes, offering principles that leave room for individual application. In essence, Scripture tells us to follow the major guidelines regarding giving, saving, and spending. Beyond that, let the Holy Spirit be your guide. Let Him help you make the delicate decisions about what you buy and how you live. Only He has the ability to factor in your unique personality, profession, gifts, and stewardship abilities.

## Putting Yourself in the Picture

Challenge group members to take time in the coming week to use part or all of this application section as an opportunity for continued growth.

# ADDITIONAL WILLOW CREEK RESOURCES

### Small Group Resources

*Coaching Life-Changing Small Group Leaders,* by Bill Donahue and Greg Bowman
*The Complete Book of Questions,* by Garry Poole
*The Connecting Church,* by Randy Frazee
*Leading Life-Changing Small Groups,* by Bill Donahue and the Willow Creek Team
*The Seven Deadly Sins of Small Group Ministry,* by Bill Donahue and Russ Robinson
*Walking the Small Group Tightrope,* by Bill Donahue and Russ Robinson

### Evangelism Resources

*Becoming a Contagious Christian* (book), by Bill Hybels and Mark Mittelberg
*The Case for a Creator,* by Lee Strobel
*The Case for Christ,* by Lee Strobel
*The Case for Faith,* by Lee Strobel
*Seeker Small Groups,* by Garry Poole
*The Three Habits of Highly Contagious Christians,* by Garry Poole

### Spiritual Gifts and Ministry

*Network Revised* (training course), by Bruce Bugbee and Don Cousins
*The Volunteer Revolution,* by Bill Hybels
*What You Do Best in the Body of Christ—Revised,* by Bruce Bugbee

### Marriage and Parenting

*Fit to Be Tied,* by Bill and Lynne Hybels
*Surviving a Spiritual Mismatch in Marriage,* by Lee and Leslie Strobel

### Ministry Resources

*An Hour on Sunday,* by Nancy Beach
*Building a Church of Small Groups,* by Bill Donahue and Russ Robinson
*The Heart of the Artist,* by Rory Noland
*Making Your Children's Ministry the Best Hour of Every Kid's Week,* by Sue Miller and David Staal
*Thriving as an Artist in the Church,* by Rory Noland

### Curriculum

*An Ordinary Day with Jesus,* by John Ortberg and Ruth Haley Barton
*Becoming a Contagious Christian* (kit), by Mark Mittelberg, Lee Strobel, and Bill Hybels
*Good Sense Budget Course,* by Dick Towner, John Tofilon, and the Willow Creek Team
*If You Want to Walk on Water, You've Got to Get Out of the Boat,* by John Ortberg with Stephen and Amanda Sorenson
*The Life You've Always Wanted,* by John Ortberg with Stephen and Amanda Sorenson
*The Old Testament Challenge,* by John Ortberg with Kevin and Sherry Harney, Mindy Caliguire, and Judson Poling

# WILLOW
### Willow Creek Association

## Willow Creek Association
*Vision, Training, Resources for Prevailing Churches*

This resource was created to serve you and to help you build a local church that prevails. It is just one of many ministry tools that are part of the Willow Creek Resources® line, published by the Willow Creek Association together with Zondervan.

The Willow Creek Association (WCA) was created in 1992 to serve a rapidly growing number of churches from across the denominational spectrum that are committed to helping unchurched people become fully devoted followers of Christ. Membership in the WCA now numbers over 10,500 Member Churches worldwide from more than ninety denominations.

The Willow Creek Association links like-minded Christian leaders with each other and with strategic vision, training, and resources in order to help them build prevailing churches designed to reach their redemptive potential. Here are some of the ways the WCA does that.

- **A2: Building Prevailing Acts 2 Churches—Today**—an annual two-and-a-half day event, held at Willow Creek Community Church in South Barrington, Illinois, to explore strategies for building churches that reach out to seekers and build believers, and to discover new innovations and breakthroughs from Acts 2 churches around the country.

- **The Leadership Summit**—a once a year, two-and-a-half-day conference to envision and equip Christians with leadership gifts and responsibilities. Presented live at Willow Creek as well as via satellite broadcast to over one hundred locations across North America, this event is designed to increase the leadership effectiveness of pastors, ministry staff, volunteer church leaders, and Christians in the marketplace.

- **Ministry-Specific Conferences**—throughout each year the WCA hosts a variety of conferences and training events—both at Willow Creek's main campus and offsite, across the U.S., and around the world—targeting church leaders and volunteers in ministry-specific areas such as: evangelism, small groups, preaching and teaching, the arts, children, students, women, volunteers, stewardship, raising up resources, etc.

- **Willow Creek Resources®**—provides churches with trusted and field-tested ministry resources in such areas as leadership, evangelism, spiritual formation, spiritual gifts, small groups, stewardship, student ministry, children's ministry, the use of the arts-drama, media, contemporary music —and more.

- **WCA Member Benefits**—includes substantial discounts to WCA training events, a 20 percent discount on all Willow Creek Resources®, *Defining Moments* monthly audio journal for leaders, quarterly *Willow* magazine, access to a Members-Only section on WillowNet, monthly communications, and more. Member Churches also receive special discounts and premier services through WCA's growing number of ministry partners—Select Service Providers—and save an average of $500 annually depending on the level of engagement.

For specific information about WCA conferences, resources, membership, and other ministry services contact:

**Willow Creek Association**
P.O. Box 3188
Barrington, IL 60011-3188
Phone: 847-570-9812
Fax: 847-765-5046
www.willowcreek.com

## Continue building your new community!
# New Community Series
### BILL HYBELS AND JOHN ORTBERG
### with Kevin and Sherry Harney

**Exodus:** *Journey Toward God* 0-310-22771-2

**Parables:** *Imagine Life God's Way* 0-310-22881-6

**Sermon on the Mount[1]:** *Connect with God* 0-310-22884-0

**Sermon on the Mount[2]:** *Connect with Others* 0-310-22883-2

**Acts:** *Build Community* 0-310-22770-4

**Romans:** *Find Freedom* 0-310-22765-8

**Philippians:** *Run the Race* 0-310-22766-6

**Colossians:** *Discover the New You* 0-310-22769-0

**James:** *Live Wisely* 0-310-22767-4

**1 Peter:** *Stand Strong* 0-310-22773-9

**1 John:** *Love Each Other* 0-310-22768-2

**Revelation:** *Experience God's Power* 0-310-22882-4

*Look for New Community at your local Christian bookstore.*

## Continue the Transformation
# Pursuing Spiritual Transformation
### JOHN ORTBERG, LAURIE PEDERSON,
### AND JUDSON POLING

**Grace:** *An Invitation to a Way of Life* 0-310-22074-2

**Growth:** *Training vs. Trying* 0-310-22075-0

**Groups:** *The Life-Giving Power of Community* 0-310-22076-9

**Gifts:** *The Joy of Serving God* 0-310-22077-7

**Giving:** *Unlocking the Heart of Good Stewardship* 0-310-22078-5

**Fully Devoted:** *Living Each Day in Jesus' Name* 0-310-22073-4

*Look for Pursuing Spiritual Transformation at your local Christian bookstore.*